Through the Bible with My Child
First Edition

Charles Sharman

Anchor-Cross Media
Cambridge, Massachusetts
www.anchorcross.org

Anchor-Cross Media
P.O. Box 381682
Cambridge, MA 02238
www.anchorcross.org

Copyright ©2008, 2009 by Charles Sharman.

All rights reserved. Printed in the United States of America.

Anchor-Cross Media is a division of Anchor-Cross Ministries, Inc.

Unless otherwise indicated, all Scripture quotations are from The Holy Bible, English Standard Version, Copyright ©2001 by Crossway Bibles, a publishing ministry of Good News Publishers. Used by permission. All rights reserved.

100% of the author's profits from this book support the ministries of Good News for India (www.goodnewsforindia.org).

This work may be copied, reproduced, transmitted, or altered for non-commercial purposes only. If it is altered, transformed, or built upon, it must be distributed under the same conditions. For the exact Legal Code, refer to the Creative Commons Attribution-Noncommercial-Share Alike 3.0 Unported license.

ISBN 978-0-9742727-1-9

Contents

I   Overview   **5**
    1   Acknowledgements 6
    2   Motivation 6
    3   Philosophy 6
    4   Overview 8
    5   Writing 8
    6   An Example Day 11
    7   The Plan Overview 12

II   Writing   **21**

III   Year One
(Genesis through Ruth)   **117**
    8   Year One Plan 118
    9   Year One Maps and Tests 135

IV   Year Two
(1 Samuel through Nehemiah, Jeremiah, Daniel)   **181**
    10   Year Two Plan 182
    11   Year Two Maps and Tests 197

V   Year Three
(Esther through Malachi, sans Psalms, Jeremiah, Daniel, and Obadiah)   **233**
    12   Year Three Plan 234
    13   Year Three Maps and Tests 249

VI   Year Four
(Matthew through Revelation)   **287**
    14   Year Four Plan 288
    15   Year Four Maps and Tests 309

Part I

Overview

1 Acknowledgements

I thank my wife, Monica Sharman, for her compilation help, editorial help, and support. I thank Peter Mayberry and Andy Hartfield for their editorial help, Joseph Sharman for his scanning help, Steve Learned for his computer help, and Finny Kuruvilla for his publishing help. Thank you.

2 Motivation

> "He established a testimony in Jacob and appointed a law in Israel, which he commanded our fathers to teach to their children, that the next generation might know them, the children yet unborn, and arise and tell them to their children, so that they should set their hope in God and not forget the works of God, but keep his commandments; and that that they should not be like their fathers, a stubborn and rebellious generation, a generation whose heart was not steadfast, whose spirit was not faithful to God." (Psalm 78:5–8)

God entrusted parents to teach their children his word. If you are a parent, you can teach your child. God gave you the ability, and you should do it.

This plan follows the teaching I gave my children while covering the Bible at home during first through fourth grade. Each plan year fits within an academic year (172 days). I released the preliminary edition in September of 2007 as the "Parent/Child Home Bible Plan." It covered Years One through Three. The first edition, published September of 2008, corrects a number of errors in the preliminary edition, adds Year Four, replaces some Year One written tests with fill-in-the-blank tests, and adds maps.

The need for parent home Bible teaching is great. May God guide you in its use, and may God be glorified!

3 Philosophy

Scripture emphasizes two major reasons for teaching: to know the LORD (consider, for example, Jeremiah 9:23–24), and to practice righteousness (consider, for example, Titus 2:1–14). Bible teachers should aim for these goals.

Despite God's command to teach, some parents may fear their role. Consider it a book study. Parents read books to their children. They discuss them. This, in many ways, is no different. The Bible wasn't written for skilled scholars, it was written for all. You can understand much of it, and you can help your child understand much of it. There are difficult parts. Admit your inability and move on. There are plenty of perfectly understandable parts that completely challenge anyone. For example: "You therefore must be perfect, as your heavenly father is perfect." (Matthew 5:48)

Inductive Bible studies consist of three parts: observation (What does the text say?), interpretation (What does the text mean?), and application (What do I do with it?). An illustration helps.

"The word of the LORD came to Samuel: 'I regret that I have made Saul king, for he has turned back from following me and has not performed my commandments.'" (1 Samuel 15:10–11a)

From this text, valid observations are:

- The LORD spoke to Samuel.
- The LORD regretted making Saul king, because Saul didn't follow God and disobeyed God's commands.

From this text, interpretations are:

- Man can disobey God's commands.
- The LORD wants people to follow him and perform his commandments.

From this text, applications are:

- I should follow the LORD.
- I should obey the LORD's commands.

Note that observation can be done perfectly. Interpretation and application are subject to human error. This plan was designed for young children. Young children grasp observation easily; therefore, this plan stresses observation.

Parents teaching older children may still find the plan helpful. Facts are essential. However, the plan has shortcomings for older ages. Parents teaching older children should add interpretation to their study.

The plan includes tests. I chose to test for two reasons. First, testing formalizes and aids review. It drives the points closer to long-term memory. Second, testing lets me evaluate my teaching. I adjusted my approach when my child scored poorly. However, testing has one drawback: the plan becomes more of a class and less of a devotion. With tests in place, I felt awkward driving home application. I feared my children would apply the word to succeed academically. I left application outside the daily Bible studies. Others who desire more of a devotional feel are welcome to discard the tests. Calling them "reviews" may also lessen tension.

The plan skips and merges some sections. The Bible contains roughly 1100 chapters. Four 172-day years cannot span the Bible a chapter per day. Therefore, I made some omissions. Sometimes I read the omitted chapters at night to my sons, and sometimes I never covered a chapter. If your child turns to Christ, they will read the skipped chapters later. If they don't, the covered chapters adequately reveal the Bible's core content.

I skipped Psalms, because I read these to my sons during summer break. We still wanted daily Bible times, but I felt a break from the rigor was necessary.

I merged 1–2 Kings and 1–2 Chronicles. They are parallel passages; therefore, studying each individually seemed redundant. I emphasized Kings but chose the Chronicles passage when it added more.

I merged Matthew through Luke, preferring a comprehensive "Life of Christ" story. I skipped some portions of John, aiming to retain Jesus' teaching during his last few days.

Sometimes, I changed the Biblical order, preferring something a bit more chronological. For example, after 1–2 Kings, we studied Jeremiah. I wanted my sons to see just how bad things were inside Judah. It's much more apparent after studying Jeremiah. I put Daniel before Ezra because much of Daniel is narrative, and most of it comes before Ezra chronologically. I split Matthew and John so the child would get two separate gospel exposures.

4 Overview

This plan covers four years of a parent/child Bible education. It takes roughly 30 minutes per day for four school years (172 days per year). Children taking the plan must be able to read and write. Each daily lesson consists of Bible reading mixed with discussion, a writing time, and a memorization time. Tests replace memorization once every 7 days or so. Adjust it as you see fit.

Begin the lesson with prayer. Then, ask review questions. From the previous day's lesson, ask the plan questions and one or two more. Also, ask one or two questions from lessons before the previous day. Then, read the Bible section together. During the reading, pause every 5–10 verses, ask questions, and teach the text. Make sure your child understands what he or she reads. The reading time should take 15–20 minutes. After the Bible reading, record "Discoveries About God," "Discoveries About Man," "God's Commands," "Lists," "Words/Phrases," and map locations. Roughly, one discovery should be recorded each day. No more than one command should be recorded each day. No more than two words/phrases should be recorded each day. On average, two map locations should be recorded each week. The writing time should take 5 minutes. Finally, memorize together. Memorization should take 5 minutes. Close the lesson with prayer.

If you find you can't hit the time targets, you are probably studying, writing, or memorizing in more detail than planned. Hit the main points. This is only their first time through. As I taught the plan, first graders took 35–40 minutes per day; fourth graders took 20–25 minutes per day. By fourth grade, my child answered questions quickly and wrote quickly.

5 Writing

Students write in the five lined paper sections: "Discoveries About God," "Discoveries About Man," "God's Commands," "Lists," and "Words/Phrases." These sections cover all four years. The writing sections occur after the yearly summaries.

Additionally, students write in each yearly plan's maps and tests sections.

5.1 Discoveries About God

The "Discoveries About God" section lists discoveries made about God's character and actions. Sometimes these discoveries come straight from the text (observation). For example, "God created the heavens and earth" comes straight from Genesis 1:1. Other times, these discoveries come from between the lines (interpretation). For example, "God knows what will happen in the future" is a safe interpretation made after reading Genesis 16:11–12. For younger students, make most discoveries observations. Have your child list the discoveries as you progress through the Bible. For example, Day 1 covers Genesis 1:1–19. In it, you learn:

- God created the heavens and earth (Genesis 1:1).
- God has a Spirit form (Genesis 1:2).

In Genesis 1:1–19, you learn other things about God: he speaks, he created the light, land, plants, and heavenly bodies good, etc. However, keep the list brief. You're doing this every day, and you'll have more Bible sections to hit the things you miss.

Have your child write each discovery in the "Discoveries About God" section. Include the reference. Aim for one discovery about God every other day. Skip a line between each item. On repeated items (e.g., God knows what will happen in the future (Genesis 16:11–12)), append the new reference (e.g., Genesis 25:23) to the item. Use the skipped line for overflow.

5.2 Discoveries About Man

The "Discoveries About Man" section is very similar to the "Discoveries About God" section, except here, the discoveries focus on man's character and actions. For example, Day 2 covers Genesis 1:20—2:3. In it, you learn:

- Man was created in God's image.
- Man was given dominion over the creatures.

Write these discoveries in the "Discoveries About Man" section. Use the same format as the "Discoveries About God" section. Aim for one discovery about man every other day. Because there are two discoveries sections your child should document one discovery per day, on average.

Sometimes, it is difficult to categorize where to place a discovery. For example, "Man was created in God's image" could have been placed in the "Discoveries About God" section as: "God made man in his image." Use your best judgment. Categorization sometimes gets in the way of Bible truth. The discoveries sections aim at writing down the bigger things, the fundamental Bible truths the author aims for. Don't fret the categorization. Furthermore, some Bible truths worth documenting fit neither category. For example, in Genesis 7, God destroys all flesh in the flood. "Animals and plants suffer because of man's sin" is a valid interpretation, and a discovery worth documenting. Yet, it falls under neither discovery section. Parents may use the untitled (blank) writing section for other discoveries.

5.3 God's Commands

God delivers commands to mankind. Have your child record each command in this section. Begin with the command recipient. For example, God commanded Adam, "You may surely eat of every tree of the garden, but of the tree of the knowledge of good and evil you shall not eat." In the commands section, your child should record: "Adam — Do not eat of the tree of knowledge of good and evil. (Genesis 2:17)"

Many commands occur in some places (e.g. Exodus 20—Deuteronomy 34). I recommend you skip recording or choose one command per day through heavy-command sections.

5.4 Lists

Recording lists aids understanding, and the Bible contains many lists. When you encounter an important list, have your child record it in this section. Example lists include The Days of Creation, The Family Line from Adam to Noah, The Ten Commandments, etc.

5.5 Words/Phrases

During Bible reading, children encounter words or phrases they don't know. Choose difficult words from the day's reading. Keep a dictionary handy. Have your child write the difficult words and their definitions in this section. Don't record more than two words per day. Missed words recur.

5.6 Untitled

A series of untitled pages follow the "Words/Phrases" section. These are for parents who want to expand the plan and add sections of their own. For example, some parents may want to add "Family Lines" or "Discoveries About Nature."

5.7 Maps

Each yearly plan includes unlabeled maps. Have your child mark major locations. On average, record two locations per week. To know the locations, you need your own Study Bible maps, Bible Atlas, or other reference.

5.8 Tests

Each yearly plan includes tests. Tests replace memorization every seven days or so. The recommended testing day can be found in the yearly plan reading and question section.

6 An Example Day

Examples clarify. My teaching style for Day 8 from Year One (Genesis 7:1—8:19) follows. Adjust it to your teaching style and your child's learning style.

- I open in prayer.

- I ask review questions from the previous day.

  Why was God sorry he had made man?

  What did God plan to do, because of man's wickedness?

  Who found favor in God's eyes?

  What did God command Noah to do?

- I say, "Please open your Bible to Genesis 7." I read 7:1–5. At the end, I ask, "What was to go on the ark?" If they don't know, I'd answer for a younger child. For an older child, I'd say, "Look at verse one. Who was supposed to go on the ark in verse one?" (I'd do the same for verses two and three.) If they still didn't get it, I'd answer. Notice there were more questions to ask from this section. I ask questions that drive at main-point observations. I usually only ask one to two questions after reading a paragraph.

- My child reads 7:6–10. At the end, I ask, "How old was Noah when the flood waters came?" I also ask, "How many days did they wait in the ark before the flood waters came?"

- I read 7:11–16. I don't ask any questions here. It reiterates 7:1–10. However, I observe: "Notice the waters came from the heavens, but they also came from within the earth."

- My child reads 7:17–24. At the end, I ask, "How high did the flood waters get?" I also ask, "What died during the flood?"

- I read 8:1–5. (Three tough words occur here: subside, abate, and recede. I briefly define each as I read.) At the end, I ask, "What happened after 150 days?"

- My child reads 8:6–12. At the end, I ask, "How did Noah discover the waters had subsided?"

- I read 8:13–19. At the end, I observe: "So, they came out of the ark." I also observe: "Let's do some math. When were the waters dry? Then look at 7:11. When did the waters start? That means the waters covered the earth for about 10 months and 13 days."

- I didn't record discoveries this day, because the section was long. However, on a regular-paced day, my child records discoveries. I'd say, "Open to the 'Discoveries About God' section. Write down, 'God destroyed the earth with a flood. (Gen. 7)'"

- My child records words/phrases. I say, "Now, open to the words/phrases section. Write down 'abate'. Abate means, 'to put an end to.'"
- We memorize together. I say, "Close your Bible. Let's continue memorizing Genesis 6:5–8 together."
- I close in prayer.

7 The Plan Overview

Consult the "Year One" plan. The plan divides the Bible across four school years. Each day's reading is shown, followed by observation questions. Typically four to eight questions are needed to grasp the main points of 20 narrative verses. However, four to eight questions daily accumulate fast, and testing becomes difficult. Instead, I recorded around two observation questions per day for testing. During the day's teaching, focus on questions beyond the two listed so the child grasps all the main points. Writing summary questions for Proverbs proved difficult. For some parts of the Bible, I used few summary questions.

Ideally, parents should derive their own daily questions. However, creating tests takes time. If you want to use the plan's written tests, you must cover the plan's questions. If you have time to create your own tests, feel free to derive your own questions.

Some days append <u>Test</u> or *Memorization* to the end. On test days, I tested my child. The referenced test is found later in the plan. On memorization days, I began memorizing a new section with my child. For example, in Year One, we began memorizing Genesis 6:5–8 on Day 6 and finished by Day 15. I memorized every day except test days. Memorization pace varies from child to child. If your child memorizes faster than mine, add other memorization sections. If your child memorizes slower than mine, skip some memorization sections. I memorized all sections along with my child.

The English Standard Version (ESV) served as this plan's Bible version. Other versions are fine, but the tests were written with the ESV's wording in mind.

A summary of the Year One through Year Four plans follows. The initial itemized number indicates the day. The summary only lists the Biblical texts covered; it skips tests, memorization references, and tested questions. Sometimes a test consumed the entire day; no time remained for Bible study. Those days are skipped in the summary. Feel free to skip Bible study if the test goes too long. Some years (particularly Year One) cover less than 172 days, anticipating some test-only days. The entire Year One through Year Four plans follow the writing sections.

7.1 Year One Summary

1. Genesis 1:1–19
2. Genesis 1:20—2:3
3. Genesis 2:4–25
4. Genesis 3
5. Genesis 4:1–16
6. Genesis 5
7. Genesis 6
8. Genesis 7:1—8:19
9. Genesis 8:20—9:17
10. Genesis 9:28—10:32
11. Genesis 11:1–26
12. Genesis 11:27—12:20
13. Genesis 14
14. Genesis 15
15. Genesis 16
16. Genesis 17:1–21
17. Genesis 18:1–21
18. Genesis 19:1–11, 23–29
19. Genesis 21
20. Genesis 22:1–19
21. Genesis 24:1–28
22. Genesis 25:1–11, 19–34
23. Genesis 26
24. Genesis 27:1–45
25. Genesis 27:46—28:22
26. Genesis 29:1–30
27. Genesis 29:31—30:24
28. Genesis 32–33
29. Genesis 34
30. Genesis 35
31. Genesis 37
32. Genesis 39
33. Genesis 40
34. Genesis 41
35. Genesis 42
36. Genesis 43
37. Genesis 44–45
38. Genesis 46
39. Genesis 47:27—48:22
40. Genesis 49
41. Genesis 50
42. Exodus 1
43. Exodus 2
44. Exodus 3
45. Exodus 4
46. Exodus 5:1—6:13
47. Exodus 7
48. Exodus 8
49. Exodus 9
50. Exodus 10
51. Exodus 11:1—12:42
52. Exodus 12:43—13:22
53. Exodus 14:1—15:21
54. Exodus 15:22—16:36
55. Exodus 17
56. Exodus 18
57. Exodus 19:1—20:21
58. Exodus 20:22–26, 22:16—23:19
59. Exodus 24
60. Exodus 25:1–40, 26:31–35
61. Exodus 28:1–14, 29:1–14
62. Exodus 29:38–46, 31
63. Exodus 32
64. Exodus 33
65. Exodus 34
66. Exodus 35:1–29
67. Exodus 35:30—36:38, 38:21–31, 39:32–43
68. Exodus 40
69. Leviticus 1–2
70. Leviticus 5:1—6:7
71. Leviticus 8
72. Leviticus 9–10
73. Leviticus 11
74. Leviticus 16
75. Leviticus 17
76. Leviticus 19
77. Leviticus 23
78. Leviticus 25
79. Leviticus 26
80. Numbers 1
81. Numbers 3
82. Numbers 6
83. Numbers 7:1–17, 9
84. Numbers 10
85. Numbers 11–12
86. Numbers 13

87. Numbers 14
88. Numbers 16
89. Numbers 17–18
90. Numbers 20
91. Numbers 21
92. Numbers 22
93. Numbers 23–24
94. Numbers 25
95. Numbers 26
96. Numbers 27
97. Numbers 30
98. Numbers 31
99. Numbers 32
100. Numbers 33:50—34:29
101. Numbers 35
102. Deuteronomy 1
103. Deuteronomy 2
104. Deuteronomy 3
105. Deuteronomy 4
106. Deuteronomy 5
107. Deuteronomy 6
108. Deuteronomy 7:1—8:10
109. Deuteronomy 9
110. Deuteronomy 10
111. Deuteronomy 11
112. Deuteronomy 12:1–28
113. Deuteronomy 14
114. Deuteronomy 15
115. Deuteronomy 16–17
116. Deuteronomy 18
117. Deuteronomy 20
118. Deuteronomy 21
119. Deuteronomy 22
120. Deuteronomy 24
121. Deuteronomy 27:1—28:14
122. Deuteronomy 28:15–48
123. Deuteronomy 29
124. Deuteronomy 30
125. Deuteronomy 31
126. Deuteronomy 32:1–47
127. Deuteronomy 32:48—34:12

128. Joshua 1
129. Joshua 2
130. Joshua 3–4
131. Joshua 5–6
132. Joshua 7
133. Joshua 8
134. Joshua 9
135. Joshua 10
136. Joshua 11
137. Joshua 13
138. Joshua 14
139. Joshua 15
140. Joshua 16–17
141. Joshua 18
142. Joshua 20–21
143. Joshua 22
144. Joshua 23
145. Joshua 24
146. Judges 1
147. Judges 2
148. Judges 3
149. Judges 4
150. Judges 5
151. Judges 6
152. Judges 7
153. Judges 8
154. Judges 9
155. Judges 11
156. Judges 13
157. Judges 14
158. Judges 15
159. Judges 16
160. Judges 17–18
161. Judges 19:1—20:11
162. Judges 20:12–48
163. Judges 21
164. Ruth 1
165. Ruth 2
166. Ruth 3
167. Ruth 4

7.2 Year Two Summary

1. 1 Samuel 1
2. 1 Samuel 2
3. 1 Samuel 3
4. 1 Samuel 4
5. 1 Samuel 5–6
6. 1 Samuel 7–8
7. 1 Samuel 9:1—10:16
8. 1 Samuel 10:17—11:15
9. 1 Samuel 12
10. 1 Samuel 13
11. 1 Samuel 14:1–46
12. 1 Samuel 14:47—15:35
13. 1 Samuel 16
14. 1 Samuel 17
15. 1 Samuel 18
16. 1 Samuel 19
17. 1 Samuel 20
18. 1 Samuel 21–22
19. 1 Samuel 23
20. 1 Samuel 24
21. 1 Samuel 25
22. 1 Samuel 26–27
23. 1 Samuel 28–29
24. 1 Samuel 30
25. 1 Samuel 31—2 Samuel 1
26. 2 Samuel 2
27. 2 Samuel 3
28. 2 Samuel 4:1—5:16
29. 2 Samuel 5:17—6:23
30. 2 Samuel 7
31. 2 Samuel 8–9
32. 2 Samuel 10
33. 2 Samuel 11
34. 2 Samuel 12
35. 2 Samuel 13
36. 2 Samuel 14
37. 2 Samuel 15
38. 2 Samuel 16–17
39. 2 Samuel 18:1—19:8
40. 2 Samuel 19:9–43
41. 2 Samuel 20:1—21:14
42. 2 Samuel 21:15—22:51
43. 2 Samuel 23
44. 2 Samuel 24
45. 1 Kings 1
46. 1 Kings 2
47. 1 Kings 3
48. 1 Kings 4
49. 1 Kings 5–6
50. 1 Kings 7
51. 1 Kings 8:1–30
52. 1 Kings 8:31–66
53. 1 Kings 9
54. 1 Kings 10
55. 1 Kings 11
56. 1 Kings 12
57. 1 Kings 13
58. 1 Kings 14
59. 2 Chronicles 11–12
60. 1 Kings 15:1–8, 2 Chronicles 13
61. 1 Kings 15:9–24, 2 Chronicles 14–16
62. 1 Kings 15:25—16:34
63. 1 Kings 17
64. 1 Kings 18
65. 1 Kings 19
66. 1 Kings 20
67. 1 Kings 21
68. 1 Kings 22:1–40
69. 2 Chronicles 17, 19
70. 2 Chronicles 20
71. 2 Kings 1
72. 2 Chronicles 21
73. 2 Kings 2
74. 2 Kings 3
75. 2 Kings 4
76. 2 Kings 5
77. 2 Kings 6:1–23
78. 2 Kings 6:24—7:20
79. 2 Kings 8
80. 2 Kings 9
81. 2 Kings 10
82. 2 Chronicles 22:10—23:21
83. 2 Chronicles 24
84. 2 Kings 13
85. 2 Chronicles 25
86. 2 Chronicles 26

87. 2 Kings 14:23—15:31
88. 2 Kings 15:32—16:20
89. 2 Kings 17
90. 2 Kings 18
91. 2 Kings 19
92. 2 Kings 20
93. 2 Kings 21
94. 2 Kings 22
95. 2 Kings 23:1–30
96. 2 Kings 23:31—24:17
97. 2 Kings 24:18—25:30
98. Jeremiah 1
99. Jeremiah 2
100. Jeremiah 4:1–26
101. Jeremiah 5
102. Jeremiah 7
103. Jeremiah 8
104. Jeremiah 9
105. Jeremiah 10
106. Jeremiah 11:18—12:17
107. Jeremiah 13
108. Jeremiah 14:1—15:4
109. Jeremiah 16
110. Jeremiah 17
111. Jeremiah 18
112. Jeremiah 19–20
113. Jeremiah 22
114. Jeremiah 23
115. Jeremiah 24:1—25:14
116. Jeremiah 26
117. Jeremiah 27
118. Jeremiah 28
119. Jeremiah 29
120. Jeremiah 30
121. Jeremiah 31
122. Jeremiah 32
123. Jeremiah 33
124. Jeremiah 34
125. Jeremiah 35
126. Jeremiah 36
127. Jeremiah 37
128. Jeremiah 38
129. Jeremiah 39
130. Jeremiah 40–41
131. Jeremiah 42–43
132. Jeremiah 44–45
133. Jeremiah 46–47
134. Jeremiah 48
135. Jeremiah 49
136. Jeremiah 50
137. Jeremiah 51
138. Jeremiah 52
139. Daniel 1
140. Daniel 2
141. Daniel 3
142. Daniel 4
143. Daniel 5
144. Daniel 6
145. Daniel 7
146. Daniel 8
147. Daniel 9
148. Daniel 10:1—11:13
149. Daniel 11:14—12:13
150. Ezra 1:1—2:39
151. Ezra 2:40—3:13
152. Ezra 4
153. Ezra 5–6
154. Ezra 7
155. Ezra 8
156. Ezra 9:1—10:17
157. Nehemiah 1–2
158. Nehemiah 3
159. Nehemiah 4
160. Nehemiah 5
161. Nehemiah 6:1—7:5
162. Nehemiah 8
163. Nehemiah 9:1–37
164. Nehemiah 10–11
165. Nehemiah 12
166. Nehemiah 13

7.3 Year Three Summary

1. Esther 1
2. Esther 2
3. Esther 3–4
4. Esther 5:1—6:13
5. Esther 6:14—8:17
6. Esther 9–10
7. Job 1
8. Job 2
9. Job 3
10. Job 4–5
11. Job 6
12. Job 7–8
13. Job 9
14. Job 10–11
15. Job 12
16. Job 13–14
17. Job 18–19
18. Job 31
19. Job 32–33
20. Job 34
21. Job 38
22. Job 39–40
23. Job 41
24. Job 42
25. Proverbs 1
26. Proverbs 2
27. Proverbs 3
28. Proverbs 4
29. Proverbs 5
30. Proverbs 6
31. Proverbs 7
32. Proverbs 8
33. Proverbs 9
34. Proverbs 10
35. Proverbs 11
36. Proverbs 12
37. Proverbs 13
38. Proverbs 15
39. Proverbs 16
40. Proverbs 17
41. Proverbs 18–19
42. Proverbs 20
43. Proverbs 21
44. Proverbs 23
45. Proverbs 24
46. Proverbs 26–27
47. Proverbs 28–29
48. Proverbs 30
49. Proverbs 31
50. Ecclesiastes 1
51. Ecclesiastes 2
52. Ecclesiastes 3
53. Ecclesiastes 4–5
54. Ecclesiastes 6:1—7:13
55. Ecclesiastes 7:14—8:17
56. Ecclesiastes 9
57. Ecclesiastes 10
58. Ecclesiastes 11–12
59. Song of Solomon 1–2
60. Song of Solomon 3–4
61. Song of Solomon 5–6
62. Song of Solomon 7–8
63. Isaiah 1
64. Isaiah 2
65. Isaiah 3–4
66. Isaiah 5
67. Isaiah 6–7
68. Isaiah 8
69. Isaiah 9
70. Isaiah 10
71. Isaiah 11–12
72. Isaiah 13
73. Isaiah 14
74. Isaiah 17–18
75. Isaiah 22
76. Isaiah 23
77. Isaiah 24
78. Isaiah 25–26
79. Isaiah 28
80. Isaiah 29
81. Isaiah 30
82. Isaiah 32
83. Isaiah 33
84. Isaiah 36
85. Isaiah 37
86. Isaiah 38–39

87. Isaiah 40
88. Isaiah 41
89. Isaiah 42
90. Isaiah 44
91. Isaiah 45
92. Isaiah 46–47
93. Isaiah 49
94. Isaiah 50–51
95. Isaiah 52–53
96. Isaiah 54–55
97. Isaiah 56–57
98. Isaiah 58
99. Isaiah 59
100. Isaiah 60
101. Isaiah 61–62
102. Isaiah 63–64
103. Isaiah 65
104. Isaiah 66
105. Lamentations 1
106. Lamentations 2
107. Lamentations 3
108. Lamentations 4–5
109. Ezekiel 1–2
110. Ezekiel 3
111. Ezekiel 4–5
112. Ezekiel 6–7
113. Ezekiel 8–9
114. Ezekiel 10
115. Ezekiel 11
116. Ezekiel 12
117. Ezekiel 13
118. Ezekiel 14–15
119. Ezekiel 16
120. Ezekiel 17
121. Ezekiel 18
122. Ezekiel 20
123. Ezekiel 22
124. Ezekiel 23
125. Ezekiel 24
126. Ezekiel 25–26
127. Ezekiel 29–30
128. Ezekiel 33
129. Ezekiel 34
130. Ezekiel 36
131. Ezekiel 37
132. Ezekiel 38–39
133. Ezekiel 40
134. Ezekiel 43
135. Ezekiel 44
136. Ezekiel 47–48
137. Hosea 1:1—2:13
138. Hosea 2:14—3:5
139. Hosea 4
140. Hosea 5:1—6:3
141. Hosea 6:4—7:16
142. Hosea 8:1—9:9
143. Hosea 9:10—10:15
144. Hosea 11–12
145. Hosea 13–14
146. Joel 1
147. Joel 2
148. Joel 3
149. Amos 1–2
150. Amos 3–4
151. Amos 5
152. Amos 6–7
153. Amos 8–9
154. Jonah 1–2
155. Jonah 3–4
156. Micah 1–2
157. Micah 3–4
158. Micah 5–6
159. Nahum 1–2
160. Nahum 3
161. Habakkuk 1:1—2:5
162. Habakkuk 2:6—3:19
163. Zephaniah 1–2
164. Zephaniah 3
165. Haggai 1–2
166. Zechariah 1–2
167. Zechariah 3–4
168. Zechariah 7–8
169. Zechariah 9–10
170. Zechariah 11
171. Zechariah 12–13
172. Malachi 1–2
173. Malachi 3–4

7.4 Year Four Summary

1. Luke 1:1–38
2. Luke 1:39–80
3. Matthew 1
4. Luke 2:1–40
5. Luke 2:41–52, Matthew 2
6. Matthew 3
7. Matthew 4
8. Matthew 5
9. Matthew 6
10. Matthew 7
11. Matthew 8
12. Matthew 9
13. Matthew 10
14. Matthew 11
15. Matthew 12:1–37
16. Matthew 12:38—13:23
17. Matthew 13:24–58
18. Matthew 14
19. Matthew 15
20. Matthew 16
21. Matthew 17
22. Matthew 18
23. Luke 15
24. Luke 16
25. Matthew 19
26. Matthew 20
27. Matthew 21
28. Matthew 22
29. Matthew 23
30. Matthew 24
31. Matthew 25
32. Matthew 26:1–35
33. Matthew 26:36–75
34. Matthew 27:1–31
35. Matthew 27:32–66
36. Matthew 28
37. Luke 24
38. Acts 1
39. Acts 2
40. Acts 3
41. Acts 4
42. Acts 5
43. Acts 6–7
44. Acts 8
45. Acts 9
46. Acts 10
47. Acts 11:19—12:25
48. Acts 13
49. Acts 14
50. Acts 15
51. Acts 16
52. Acts 17
53. Acts 18
54. Acts 19
55. Acts 20
56. Acts 21:1–36
57. Acts 21:37—22:29
58. Acts 22:30—23:35
59. Acts 24:1—25:12
60. Acts 25:13—26:32
61. Acts 27
62. Acts 28
63. Romans 1
64. Romans 2
65. Romans 3
66. Romans 4
67. Romans 5:1—6:14
68. Romans 6:15—7:25
69. Romans 8
70. Romans 9:1–29
71. Romans 9:30—10:21
72. Romans 11
73. Romans 12
74. Romans 13–14
75. Romans 15
76. Romans 16
77. 1 Corinthians 1
78. 1 Corinthians 2–3
79. 1 Corinthians 4
80. 1 Corinthians 5–6
81. 1 Corinthians 7
82. 1 Corinthians 8–9
83. 1 Corinthians 10
84. 1 Corinthians 11
85. 1 Corinthians 12–13
86. 1 Corinthians 14

87. 1 Corinthians 15
88. 2 Corinthians 1–2
89. 2 Corinthians 3–4
90. 2 Corinthians 5
91. 2 Corinthians 6–7
92. 2 Corinthians 8–9
93. 2 Corinthians 11
94. 2 Corinthians 12–13
95. Galatians 1
96. Galatians 2
97. Galatians 3
98. Galatians 4
99. Galatians 5–6
100. Ephesians 1
101. Ephesians 2–3
102. Ephesians 4
103. Ephesians 5
104. Ephesians 6
105. Philippians 1
106. Philippians 2
107. Philippians 3–4
108. Colossians 1
109. Colossians 2
110. Colossians 3–4
111. 1 Thessalonians 1:1—2:16
112. 1 Thessalonians 2:17—4:12
113. 1 Thessalonians 4:13—5:28
114. 2 Thessalonians 1:1—2:12
115. 2 Thessalonians 2:13—3:18
116. 1 Timothy 1–2
117. 1 Timothy 3–4
118. 1 Timothy 5
119. 1 Timothy 6
120. 2 Timothy 1
121. 2 Timothy 2
122. 2 Timothy 3–4
123. Titus 1–2
124. Titus 3–Philemon
125. John 1:1–34
126. John 3
127. John 4:1–42
128. John 6:22–71
129. John 9
130. John 11
131. John 13
132. John 14
133. John 15
134. John 16
135. John 17
136. John 18
137. John 19
138. John 20
139. John 21
140. Hebrews 1–2
141. Hebrews 3:1—4:13
142. Hebrews 4:14—6:20
143. Hebrews 9
144. Hebrews 10
145. Hebrews 11
146. Hebrews 12
147. Hebrews 13
148. James 1
149. James 2
150. James 3–4
151. James 5
152. 1 Peter 1
153. 1 Peter 2
154. 1 Peter 3
155. 1 Peter 4–5
156. 2 Peter 1
157. 2 Peter 2
158. 2 Peter 3
159. 1 John 1:1—2:17
160. 1 John 2:18—3:24
161. 1 John 4
162. 1 John 5
163. Jude
164. Revelation 1
165. Revelation 2
166. Revelation 3
167. Revelation 4–5
168. Revelation 6–7
169. Revelation 8–9
170. Revelation 10–11
171. Revelation 12–13
172. Revelation 14–15
173. Revelation 19–20
174. Revelation 21
175. Revelation 22

Part II

Writing

Discoveries About God

Discoveries About God

Discoveries About God

Discoveries About God

Discoveries About God

Discoveries About God

Discoveries About God

Discoveries About God

Discoveries About God

Discoveries About God

Discoveries About God

Discoveries About God

Discoveries About God

Discoveries About God

Discoveries About God

Discoveries About God

Discoveries About God

Discoveries About God

Discoveries About God

Discoveries About God

Discoveries About God

Discoveries About God

Discoveries About God

Discoveries About God

Discoveries About Man

Discoveries About Man

Discoveries About Man

Discoveries About Man

Discoveries About Man

Discoveries About Man

Discoveries About Man

Discoveries About Man

Discoveries About Man

Discoveries About Man

Discoveries About Man

Discoveries About Man

Discoveries About Man

Discoveries About Man

Discoveries About Man

Discoveries About Man

Discoveries About Man

Discoveries About Man

Discoveries About Man

Discoveries About Man

God's Commands

God's Commands

God's Commands

God's Commands

God's Commands

God's Commands

God's Commands

God's Commands

God's Commands

God's Commands

God's Commands

God's Commands

Lists

Lists

Lists

Lists

Lists

Lists

Lists

Lists

Lists

Lists

Words/Phrases

Words/Phrases

Words/Phrases

Words/Phrases

Words/Phrases

Words/Phrases

Words/Phrases

Words/Phrases

Words/Phrases

Words/Phrases

Words/Phrases

Words/Phrases

Words/Phrases

Words/Phrases

Words/Phrases

Words/Phrases

Words/Phrases

Words/Phrases

Words/Phrases

Words/Phrases

Part III

Year One
(Genesis through Ruth)

8 Year One Plan

1. Genesis 1:1–19   *Memorize* Creation Days 1–7

2. Genesis 1:20—2:3

    (a) All that God had made was very ____.

3. Genesis 2:4–25

    (a) From what did God make man?

    (b) From what did God make woman?

4. Genesis 3

    (a) What one command did God have for the man and woman?

    (b) What curses did God make when man disobeyed?

5. Genesis 4:1–16   <u>Test</u>: Genesis 1

    (a) What are the names of Adam and Eve's first two sons?

    (b) What did Cain do to Abel?

6. Genesis 5   *Memorize* Genesis 6:5–8

    (a) What happened to Enoch?

    (b) Who were Noah's three sons?

7. Genesis 6   <u>Test</u>: Genesis 2–5

    (a) Why was God sorry he had made man?

    (b) Who found favor in God's eyes?

8. Genesis 7:1—8:19

    (a) How old was Noah when the flood waters came?

    (b) Who and what died during the flood?

9. Genesis 8:20—9:17

    (a) What did Noah build after coming from the ark?

    (b) What is special about the rainbow?

10. Genesis 9:28—10:32

11. Genesis 11:1–26

    (a) What did man do at Babel?

(b) What did God do at Babel?

12. Genesis 11:27—12:20

    (a) What did God ask Abram to do?

    (b) What did God promise Abram?

13. Genesis 14   <u>Test</u>: Genesis 6–11

    (a) What did Melchizedek do for Abram?

    (b) What happened to Lot, after he was captured by the four kings?

14. Genesis 15

    (a) How many offspring would Abram have?

    (b) For how many years would Abram's offspring be afflicted?

15. Genesis 16   *Memorize* Genesis 12:1–3

    (a) Who was Ishmael?

    (b) Who met Hagar in the wilderness?

16. Genesis 17:1–21

    (a) Why was Abram's name changed to Abraham?

    (b) How was Abraham to keep God's covenant?

17. Genesis 18:1–21

    (a) Why did Sarah laugh?

    (b) Why was Abraham chosen?

18. Genesis 19:1–11, 23–29

    (a) Why did God destroy Sodom and Gomorrah?

    (b) Who was spared?

19. Genesis 21   <u>Test</u>: Genesis 12–18

    (a) What does Isaac mean?

    (b) Why did Hagar and Ishmael leave Abraham?

20. Genesis 22:1–19

    (a) What did God command Abraham to do to Isaac?

    (b) Why did Abraham call the mount of the LORD, "The LORD will provide"?

21. Genesis 24:1–28   *Memorize* Genesis 22:10–12

(a) What did Abraham ask his servant to do for Isaac?

(b) How did God answer the servant's prayer?

22. Genesis 25:1–11, 19–34

    (a) After Sarah died, Abraham took another wife. What was her name?

    (b) Why did Isaac pray to the LORD about his wife?

    (c) For what did Esau sell his birthright?

23. Genesis 26

    (a) What did God promise Isaac?

    (b) Why did Abimelech send Isaac away?

24. Genesis 27:1–45

    (a) Who told Jacob to get Esau's blessing?

    (b) How did Jacob convince Isaac he was Esau?

    (c) What did Esau plan to do to Jacob?

25. Genesis 27:46—28:22   Test: Genesis 19–26

    (a) Who told Jacob to find a wife in Paddan-aram?

    (b) Describe Jacob's dream.

    (c) How did Jacob respond to the dream?

26. Genesis 29:1–30

    (a) How many years did Jacob work for Rachel?

    (b) How did Laban deceive Jacob?

27. Genesis 29:31—30:24

    (a) Which wife bore Jacob's first four sons?

    (b) Why did Rachel give Bilhah to Jacob as a wife?

28. Genesis 32–33

    (a) Why was Jacob afraid of Esau?

    (b) How did Jacob plan to please Esau?

    (c) Jacob wrestled with a man. Why did the man change Jacob's name to Israel?

    (d) How did Esau treat Jacob?

29. Genesis 34

    (a) What did Shechem, the son of Hamor, do to Dinah?

(b) How did Simeon and Levi avenge the wrong done to their sister?

30. Genesis 35

    (a) God commanded Jacob to go to Bethel. What did Jacob command his family?

    (b) What happened to Rachel after she gave birth to Benjamin?

31. Genesis 37

    (a) Describe Joseph's two dreams.

    (b) What feelings did Joseph's brothers have towards him?

32. Genesis 39   <u>Test</u>: Genesis 27–35

    (a) How did God treat Potiphar's household while Joseph was there?

    (b) Why was Joseph thrown into prison?

33. Genesis 40

    (a) What did Joseph do for the chief cupbearer and the chief baker?

    (b) What did Joseph ask the chief cupbearer to do for him?

34. Genesis 41   *Memorize* Genesis 32:24–28

    (a) Describe Pharaoh's dreams.

    (b) Why was Joseph made second-in-command over Egypt?

    (c) Name Joseph's two sons.

35. Genesis 42

    (a) When Joseph's brothers came to buy grain the first time, how did he treat them?

    (b) Why did Joseph's brothers believe they were being treated poorly?

36. Genesis 43   <u>Test</u>: Genesis 37–41

    (a) Why did Joseph's brothers return to Egypt (the second time)?

    (b) What did Joseph do for his brothers on their return trip?

37. Genesis 44–45

    (a) Why did Joseph plan to keep Benjamin as a servant?

    (b) What did Judah offer instead?

    (c) Why did Jacob move to Egypt (two reasons)?

38. Genesis 46

    (a) What did God think about Jacob's visit to Egypt?

(b) How many belonging to Jacob came to Egypt?

39. Genesis 47:27—48:22

    (a) What two things did Jacob do for Ephraim and Manasseh?

    (b) As Jacob blessed Ephraim and Manasseh, what bothered Joseph?

40. Genesis 49

    (a) Before Jacob died, what did he do for his sons?

    (b) What did Jacob predict about Judah?

    (c) What did Jacob command his sons about his burial?

41. Genesis 50   *Memorize* Exodus 3:1–6

    (a) Why did Joseph briefly return to Canaan?

    (b) After Jacob died, what did Joseph's brothers fear?

42. Exodus 1

    (a) Why did the Egyptians treat the Israelites poorly?

    (b) After Joseph died, what did the Israelites become?

    (c) Why did God bless the midwives?

43. Exodus 2   Test: Genesis 42–50

    (a) How was Moses saved from Pharaoh?

    (b) Why did Moses flee Egypt?

    (c) How did Moses help Reuel's daughters?

44. Exodus 3

    (a) How did God first reveal himself to Moses?

    (b) Why did God ask Moses to deliver the Israelites from Egypt?

    (c) What is God's name?

45. Exodus 4

    (a) Name two reasons Moses had for not leading.

    (b) Whom did God send to help Moses?

    (c) What were the three signs God gave Moses?

46. Exodus 5:1—6:13

    (a) When Moses first spoke to Pharaoh, how did Pharaoh respond?

    (b) How did Moses and the Israelites feel after Pharaoh took the straw from them?

47. Exodus 7

   (a) What is the first miracle Moses performed in Pharaoh's presence?

   (b) Why didn't Pharaoh let the people go after witnessing a miracle?

48. Exodus 8   <u>Test</u>: Exodus 1–4

   (a) During which plague did Pharaoh first say the people could go?

   (b) After the frogs were gone, what did Pharaoh do?

49. Exodus 9

   (a) When Moses threw dust from the kiln into the air, what happened?

   (b) When the Egyptians heard hail was coming, how did they respond?

50. Exodus 10

   (a) Why did God bring an east wind on Egypt all night?

   (b) After the plague of darkness, what did Pharaoh command Moses?

51. Exodus 11:1—12:42

   (a) Name some Passover preparations.

   (b) What did God do to Egypt on Passover night?

   (c) Why did the people leave Egypt with unleavened bread?

   (d) How many years did the Israelites live in Egypt?

52. Exodus 12:43—13:22   *Memorize* The Ten Plagues

   (a) Why were the firstborn set aside for God?

   (b) In what form did God lead the Israelites out of Egypt?

53. Exodus 14:1—15:21

   (a) After the people fled Egypt, what did Pharaoh decide?

   (b) How did God save the Israelites near the Red Sea?

   (c) What did Moses and the Israelites do after God saved them from the Egyptians at the Red Sea?

54. Exodus 15:22—16:36

   (a) What was wrong with the water at Marah?

   (b) What food did God provide the Israelites for 40 years?

   (c) What were some rules about the manna?

55. Exodus 17

(a) What happened at Massah and Meribah?

(b) What did Amalek do to Israel?

56. Exodus 18   <u>Test</u>: Exodus 7–12

(a) What did Jethro declare about the LORD?

(b) How did Jethro advise Moses?

57. Exodus 19:1—20:21

(a) What did God promise if the Israelites kept God's covenant?

(b) How did God come upon Mt. Sinai?

(c) What laws did God first give Moses from Mt. Sinai?

58. Exodus 20:22–26, 22:16—23:19   <u>Test</u>: Exodus 13–18

(a) How should the Israelites treat sojourners?

(b) What three feasts were the Israelites to keep?

59. Exodus 24   *Memorize* The Ten Commandments

(a) After Moses read God's law before the people, what did they declare?

(b) What did Moses, Aaron, Nadab and Abihu see?

(c) How much time did Moses spend on Mt. Sinai?

60. Exodus 25:1–40, 26:31–35

(a) What articles went in the Holy Place of the Tabernacle?

(b) What went in the Most Holy Place of the Tabernacle?

(c) What would God do from the mercy seat?

61. Exodus 28:1–14, 29:1–14

(a) Name some garments the priests must wear.

(b) For how many days were the priests consecrated?

62. Exodus 29:38–46, 31

(a) What made up the daily sacrifice?

(b) Whom did God appoint to build the tabernacle and the other things for worshipping God?

63. Exodus 32

(a) As Moses delayed coming from the mountain, what did the people ask Aaron to do?

- (b) After the people worshipped the golden calf, what did God plan?
- (c) When Moses saw the calf and the people dancing, what did he do with the tablets?
- (d) Which tribe was on Moses' and the LORD's side?

64. Exodus 33   <u>Test</u>: Exodus 19–31

    - (a) What would the people do as Moses went to the Tent of Meeting?
    - (b) What did Moses see?

65. Exodus 34

    - (a) Name some things God declared about himself when Moses went to Sinai the second time.
    - (b) Why did Moses put a veil over his face?

66. Exodus 35:1–29   *Memorize* Exodus 40:34–38

    - (a) Who (of Israel) contributed goods for building the tabernacle and its furnishings?

67. Exodus 35:30—36:38, 38:21–31, 39:32–43

    - (a) Why did Moses tell the people to quit contributing goods for the tabernacle and its furnishings?
    - (b) How well did the people obey God in constructing the tabernacle and its furnishings?

68. Exodus 40

    - (a) Why couldn't Moses enter the tent of meeting?

69. Leviticus 1–2

    - (a) What was the burnt offering's purpose?
    - (b) What portion of the grain offering belonged to the priests?

70. Leviticus 5:1—6:7   <u>Test</u>: Exodus 32–40

    - (a) When should people offer a sin offering?
    - (b) What did the sin offering do?

71. Leviticus 8

72. Leviticus 9–10

    - (a) What did the LORD do to Aaron's first burnt offering?

(b) Nadab and Abihu offered unauthorized fire before the LORD. What happened to them?

73. Leviticus 11

    (a) What animals could Israel eat?

    (b) What fish could Israel eat?

74. Leviticus 16

    (a) What happened on the Day of Atonement (for the people and all Israel)?

    (b) What was special about the goat for Azazel?

75. Leviticus 17 *Memorize* The Five Types of Sacrifice

    (a) In what places should Israel offer sacrifices?

    (b) What part of the sacrifice atoned for sins?

76. Leviticus 19

    (a) How should you treat your neighbor?

    (b) Why should Israel be holy?

77. Leviticus 23 Test: Leviticus 1–16

    (a) Why did Israel celebrate the Feast of Booths?

78. Leviticus 25 *Memorize* Leviticus 20:26

    (a) How often did the Year of Jubilee come?

    (b) Name some things that happened in the Year of Jubilee.

79. Leviticus 26

    (a) Name some blessings God would grant if Israel obeyed his commands.

    (b) Name some punishments God would cause if Israel disobeyed his commands.

    (c) If Israel disobeyed and God punished them, was there a chance to return? How?

80. Numbers 1

    (a) Which tribe had the most men?

    (b) Which tribe took care of the tabernacle and its furnishings?

81. Numbers 3 Test: Leviticus 17–26

    (a) Who served as a substitute for the firstborn from all tribes?

82. Numbers 6 *Memorize* Numbers 6:22–27

    (a) What are the three special rules for a Nazirite?

    (b) Why does someone become a Nazirite?

83. Numbers 7:1–17, 9

    (a) How did the people offer their first sacrifices after the tabernacle was set up?

    (b) Name some things the chiefs offered.

    (c) Who determined when Israel set out and when they remained in camp?

84. Numbers 10

    (a) What was the purpose of the two silver trumpets?

    (b) What did Moses ask Hobab?

85. Numbers 11–12

    (a) How did God help Moses carry the burden of the people?

    (b) The people craved meat. What did God do?

    (c) Why should Miriam and Aaron fear to speak against Moses?

86. Numbers 13

    (a) Why did the LORD and Moses send spies to Canaan?

    (b) What report did the spies bring back?

87. Numbers 14 <u>Test</u>: Numbers 1–12

    (a) How did the people react to the spies' report?

    (b) Who warned the people not to rebel but to trust God?

    (c) What was the people's punishment?

88. Numbers 16

    (a) What did Korah and the others think Moses had done wrong?

    (b) What did God do to Korah and the others?

89. Numbers 17–18 *Memorize* Numbers 20:2–13

    (a) Aaron's staff budded with almonds. What did this mean?

    (b) What would be the Levites' inheritance?

90. Numbers 20

    (a) Why couldn't Moses and Aaron enter the promised land?

91. Numbers 21

    (a) How did God help those bitten by fiery serpents?

    (b) What did Israel do to Sihon, king of the Amorites, and Og, king of Bashan?

92. Numbers 22

    (a) Why did Balaam refuse to go with Balak?

    (b) How did Balaam's donkey save him?

    (c) What did God want Balaam to say about Israel?

93. Numbers 23–24   <u>Test</u>: Numbers 13–21

    (a) Balak asked Balaam to curse Israel. Did Balaam curse Israel?

94. Numbers 25

    (a) How did Phinehas turn back God's wrath?

95. Numbers 26

    (a) Moses and Eleazer took a second census. Who remained from the first census?

96. Numbers 27

    (a) What happened to a man's land after he died, if he had no son?

    (b) Whom did God appoint to succeed Moses?

97. Numbers 30

    (a) If a man made a vow to the LORD, what should he do?

98. Numbers 31

    (a) Why did the Israelites war against Midian?

    (b) How many warriors survived the battle?

99. Numbers 32   <u>Test</u>: Numbers 22–30

    (a) Where did Reuben, Gad and half of Manasseh want to settle?

    (b) What must they do to be allowed to settle there?

100. Numbers 33:50—34:29

    (a) How were the Israelites to divide up the land?

101. Numbers 35

    (a) How did the Levites get cities?

(b) What happened to someone who accidentally murdered someone else?

102. Deuteronomy 1

(a) Deuteronomy begins with a summary of what?

103. Deuteronomy 2

(a) What three kingdoms did Israel pass through peacefully on the way to Canaan?

104. Deuteronomy 3   <u>Test</u>: Numbers 31–35

105. Deuteronomy 4

(a) If Israel served other gods in the land, what will happen to them?

(b) Complete the statement, "You will find him, if ... "

106. Deuteronomy 5

(a) Deuteronomy 5 begins a summary of the law. What laws come first?

107. Deuteronomy 6

(a) How much should Israel love the LORD?

(b) How much should Israel study the law?

108. Deuteronomy 7:1—8:10

(a) How should Israel relate with the Canaanites?

(b) Why did God let the people hunger and provide them with manna?

109. Deuteronomy 9   <u>Test</u>: Deuteronomy 1–6

(a) Israel's righteousness was not God's motive for giving them the land. What was his reason?

(b) What was wrong with Israel's righteousness?

110. Deuteronomy 10

(a) Because God loved them, what should Israel do with their hearts?

111. Deuteronomy 11   *Memorize* Deuteronomy 6:4–9

(a) What is the blessing and the curse that Moses set before the Israelites?

(b) If Israel was careful to obey, what would God do to the Canaanite nations?

112. Deuteronomy 12:1–28

(a) When the Israelites enter the land, where should they offer sacrifices?

113. Deuteronomy 14

  (a) What made an animal clean?

  (b) The Israelites had crops and herds. What portion should they give to God?

114. Deuteronomy 15   Test: Deuteronomy 7–12

  (a) What rules did God have for lending to the poor?

115. Deuteronomy 16–17

  (a) What rules did God have for Israel's judges?

  (b) How many witnesses were needed in a court case?

116. Deuteronomy 18

  (a) Who should not be found in Israel?

  (b) How would the Israelites hear God's words after Moses' death?

117. Deuteronomy 20

  (a) Why should Israel not fear battles against larger armies?

118. Deuteronomy 21

  (a) If someone was found dead in the open country, what was done?

119. Deuteronomy 22   Test: Deuteronomy 14–20

  (a) What should an Israelite do if he saw a neighbor's ox going astray?

120. Deuteronomy 24   *Memorize* Deuteronomy 30:11–14

  (a) Why should a child not be put to death for a father's sin?

  (b) Why should farmers not pass through their fields a second time for harvest?

121. Deuteronomy 27:1—28:14

  (a) When the Israelites enter the land, what should the Israelites declare from two mountains?

  (b) When would God bless the Israelites?

  (c) Name some blessings God would give for obedience.

122. Deuteronomy 28:15–48

  (a) Why would curses come on the Israelites?

  (b) Name some curses that would come because of disobedience.

123. Deuteronomy 29

(a) What does God say about secret and revealed things?

124. Deuteronomy 30   <u>Test</u>: Deuteronomy 21–28

(a) After God's curse came, was there any hope for Israel?

(b) What choice involved the blessing and the curse?

125. Deuteronomy 31

(a) When did God want Israel to publicly read the law?

(b) What did God predict about Israel's future behavior?

126. Deuteronomy 32:1–47   *Memorize* Deuteronomy 32:1–4

(a) How are God and an eagle compared?

(b) How did Israel react to God's kindness?

127. Deuteronomy 32:48—34:12

(a) Describe Moses' body when he died.

(b) How is Moses a unique prophet?

128. Joshua 1

(a) Name some commandments God gave Joshua across the Jordan.

129. Joshua 2   <u>Test</u>: Deuteronomy 29–34

(a) How did Rahab help the spies?

(b) What did Rahab declare about the Lord?

(c) What promise did Rahab make with the spies?

130. Joshua 3–4

(a) How did the people cross the Jordan?

(b) What did the twelve stones mean?

131. Joshua 5–6

(a) Why did Joshua pause before Jericho and circumcise the Israelites?

(b) What happened on the fourteenth day of the first month on the plains of Jericho?

(c) How was Jericho taken?

(d) What curse did Joshua make about Jericho?

132. Joshua 7

(a) What did Achan do wrong?

(b) What happened to Israel because Achan sinned?

133. Joshua 8   <u>Test</u>: Joshua 1–6

(a) How did Israel conquer Ai?

(b) After the battle of Ai, what did Israel do from Mount Ebal and Mount Gerizim?

134. Joshua 9

(a) How did the Gibeonites deceive Israel?

(b) How were the Gibeonites punished?

135. Joshua 10

(a) Why did Joshua march all night to help Gibeon?

(b) How did God help Joshua in the battle of Gibeon?

136. Joshua 11   *Memorize* Joshua 10:12–14

(a) Why didn't more cities make peace with Israel?

137. Joshua 13

(a) Had the Israelites finished conquering Canaan by the time Joshua was old?

138. Joshua 14

(a) What city did the LORD give Caleb?

139. Joshua 15   <u>Test</u>: Joshua 7–13

140. Joshua 16–17

141. Joshua 18

(a) Seven tribes were slow to take their portions of the land. How did Joshua get them to do something about it?

142. Joshua 20–21

(a) How many of God's promises to Israel about the land failed?

143. Joshua 22

(a) Why did the tribes west of the Jordan prepare for war against the transjordan tribes?

(b) Why did the transjordan tribes build an altar?

144. Joshua 23   *Memorize* Joshua 23:14–16

(a) Complete Joshua's statement, "Just as God brought all these good things for you …"

145. Joshua 24

(a) Whom did Israel choose to serve?

(b) What served as a witness?

146. Judges 1

(a) Did Israel completely conquer the Canaanites?

147. Judges 2   Test: Joshua 14–24

(a) After Joshua and his generation died, a new generation arose. How well did that generation know the LORD?

(b) How did God punish Israel for going after other gods?

(c) How did God deliver Israel from their plunderers?

(d) After the judge died, how did Israel act?

148. Judges 3

(a) Othniel saved Israel from whom?

(b) How did Ehud kill Eglon?

149. Judges 4

(a) What did Deborah tell Barak?

(b) Why did God give the victory over Sisera to a woman?

150. Judges 5

151. Judges 6

(a) How did Gideon know he spoke to the angel of the LORD?

(b) Why was Gideon called Jerubbaal?

152. Judges 7   Test: Judges 1–5

(a) How did Gideon defeat Midian?

(b) How did God reduce Gideon's army?

153. Judges 8

(a) Which kings did Gideon pursue east of the Jordan?

(b) After the battle with Midian, what did Israel ask of Gideon?

(c) What did Gideon make with the Midianite gold?

154. Judges 9

　　(a) What curse did Jotham place on Abimelech and Shechem?

　　(b) How was the curse fulfilled?

155. Judges 11

　　(a) Why was Jephthah driven from his home?

　　(b) What vow did Jephthah make?

156. Judges 13　　　　　　　　　　　　　　　　　　　　*Memorize* Judges 7:19–22

　　(a) What did the angel tell Manoah's wife?

　　(b) What was the angel's name?

157. Judges 14　　　　　　　　　　　　　　　　　　　　<u>Test</u>: Judges 6–11

　　(a) Whom did Samson want to marry?

　　(b) What was Samson's riddle?

158. Judges 15

　　(a) Why did Samson burn the grain fields of the Philistines?

　　(b) How did God help Samson after his victory with the jawbone?

159. Judges 16

　　(a) What was the secret of Samson's strength?

　　(b) Who discovered the secret?

　　(c) How did Samson die?

160. Judges 17–18

　　(a) What did Micah's mother make?

　　(b) What did the Danites take from Micah?

161. Judges 19:1—20:11

　　(a) What evil befell a Levite and his concubine in Gibeah?

　　(b) What did Israel plan to do about it?

162. Judges 20:12–48

　　(a) Did Benjamin give up the men of Gibeah to be punished by Israel?

　　(b) How many times did Benjamin defeat Israel, before Israel defeated them?

163. Judges 21

(a) How did Benjamin get wives?

164. Ruth 1

    (a) What did Naomi lose in Moab?

    (b) What was Ruth determined to do?

165. Ruth 2 Test: Judges 13–21

    (a) In what field did Ruth glean?

    (b) How did Boaz treat Ruth?

166. Ruth 3

    (a) Boaz ate, drank and lay down. What did Ruth do that night?

    (b) What did Boaz promise next?

167. Ruth 4 Test: Ruth

    (a) Who witnessed Boaz's purchase of Naomi's property?

    (b) What was the name of Boaz and Ruth's son?

9 Year One Maps and Tests

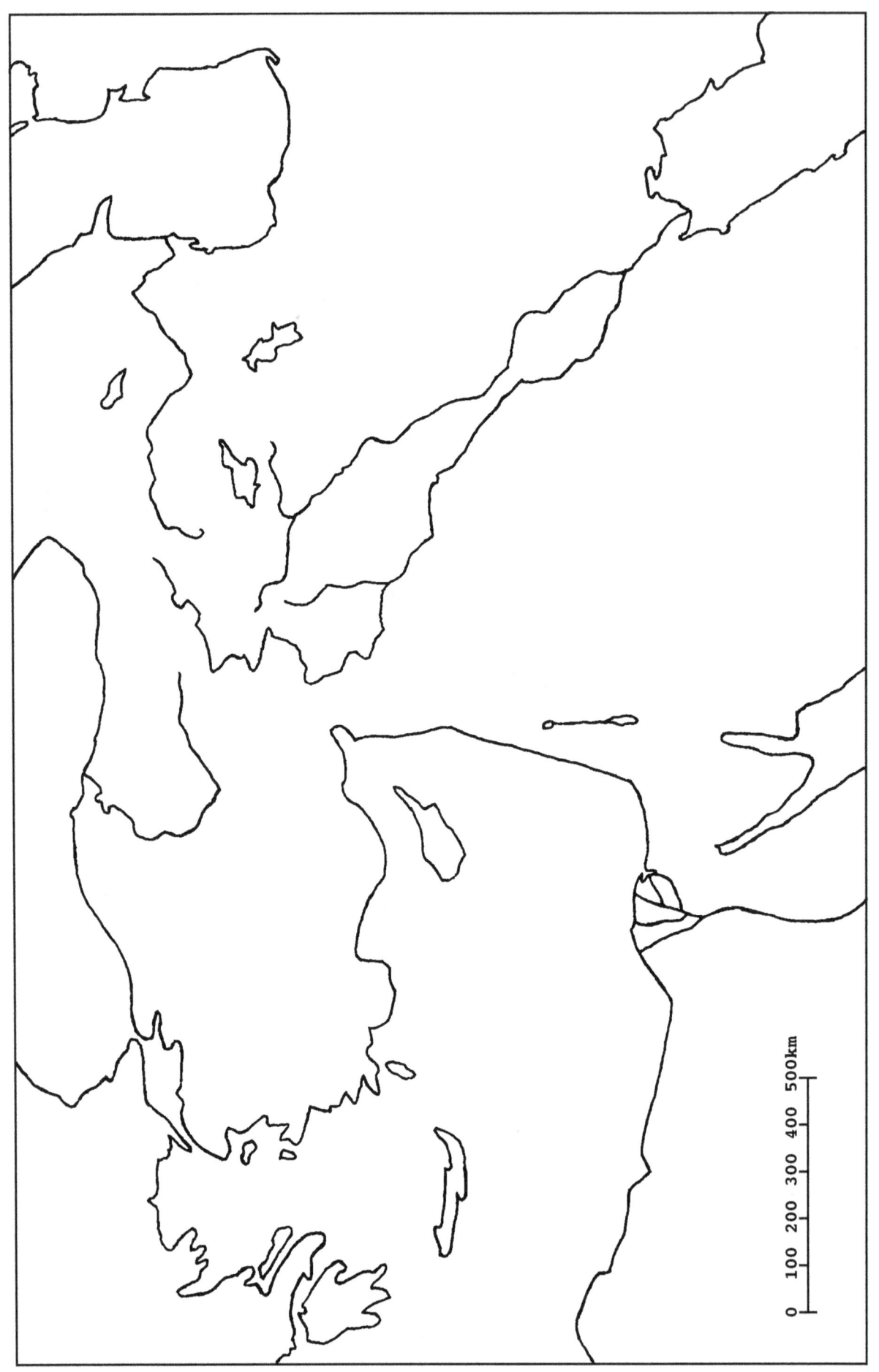

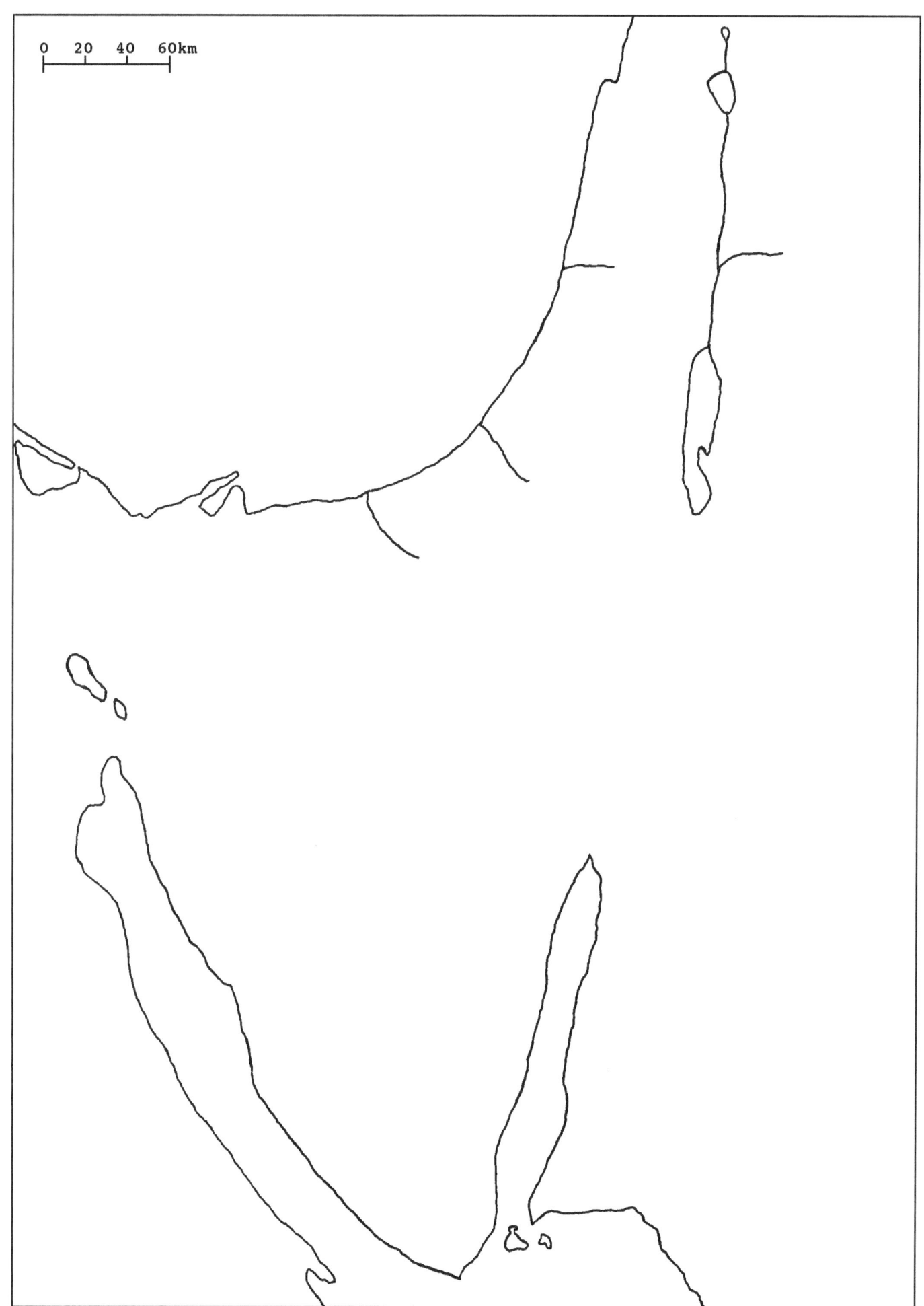

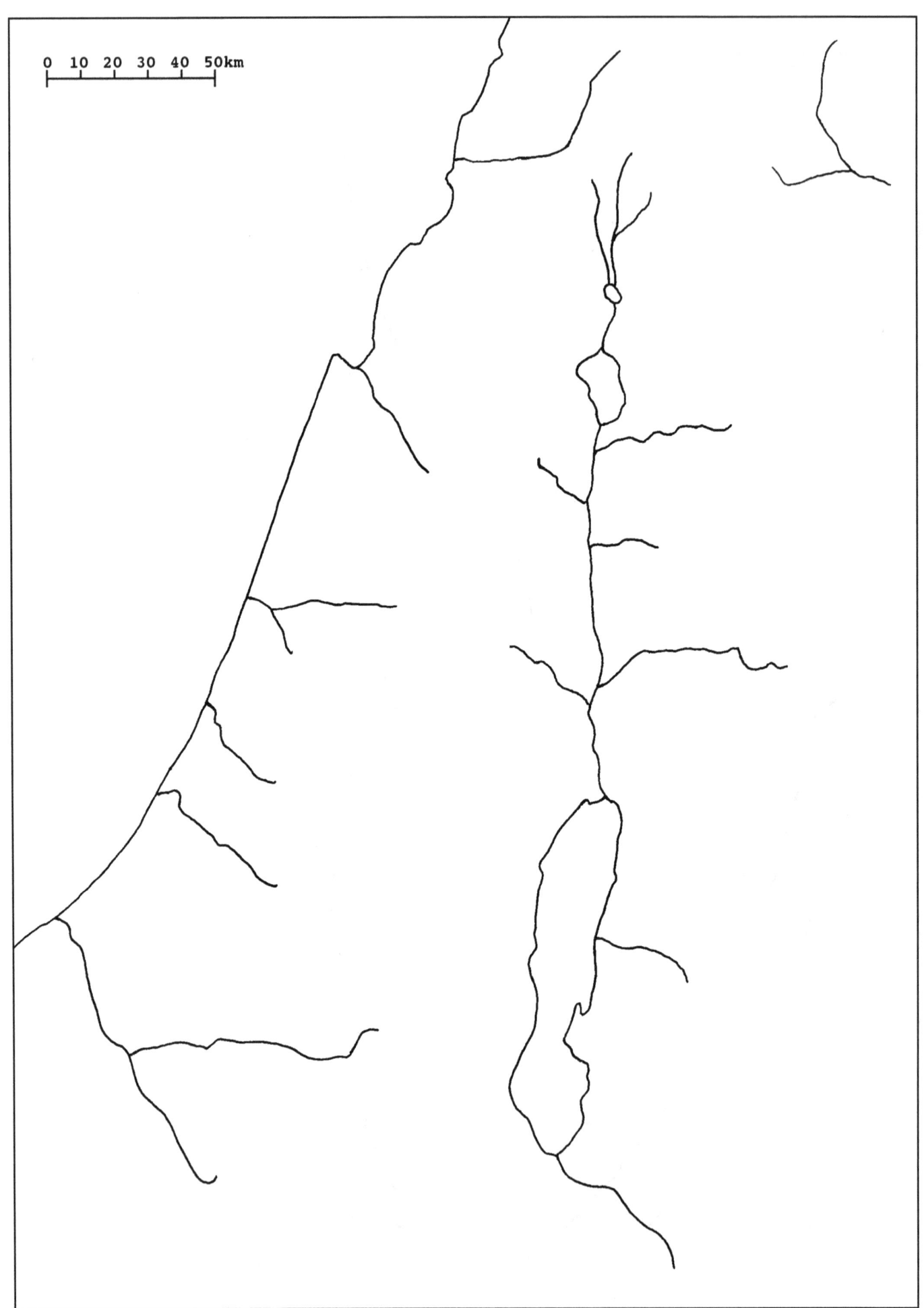

Genesis 1

Write what God did on each day of creation.

Day 1 _____

Day 2 _____

Day 3 _____

Day 4 _____

Day 5 _____

Day 6 _____

Day 7 _____

Genesis 2–5

Directions: Circle the letter of the best answer.

1. From what did God make man?

    (a) flesh

    (b) apes

    (c) a rib

    (d) dust

2. What command did God have for Adam and Eve?

    (a) Bring sacrifices to me.

    (b) Do not eat from the tree of knowledge of good and evil.

    (c) Do not eat from the tree of life.

    (d) Love the LORD.

3. What curses did God make when man disobeyed?

    (a) serpent: crawl on belly; woman: pain in childbirth; man: work the ground

    (b) serpent: death; woman: pain in childbirth; man: poverty

    (c) serpent: crawl on belly; woman: hatred for others; man: lose eyesight

    (d) serpent: eat grass; woman: have no children; man: death

4. What are the names of Adam and Eve's first two sons?

    (a) Bill and Steve

    (b) Cain and Seth

    (c) Cain and Abel

    (d) Abel and Seth

5. What did Cain do?

    (a) hugged his mother

    (b) gave gifts to the poor

    (c) murdered his brother

    (d) hated the LORD

6. What happened to Enoch?

    (a) God took him away.

    (b) God punished him.

    (c) He was drowned in a flood.

    (d) God blessed him with many sheep.

7. Who were Noah's three sons?

    (a) Shem, Ham and Jared

    (b) Sam, Heber and Japheth

    (c) Shem, Haran and Josiah

    (d) Shem, Ham and Japheth

Genesis 6–11

Directions: Fill in the blanks.

1. Noah was _____ years old when the flood waters came.

2. During the flood, _____ living thing that moved on the earth died. Only Noah and those on the ark were left.

3. Noah built an _____ after coming from the ark.

4. The _____ is a sign that God will never again destroy the earth with a flood.

5. At Babel, man tried to build a _____ with its top in the heavens.

6. God confused man's _____ at Babel.

The Call of Abram (Genesis 12–18)

Across
2 Sarah _____ because she was too old to bear children.
4 Abram _____ Lot from the four kings.
7 What word means "father of many"?
9 Where did God ask Abram to go?
11 Abram's offspring would be as many as the _____.
12 Who met Hagar in the wilderness?

Down
1 Melchizedek _____ Abram.
3 How was Abraham to keep God's covenant?
5 Abram's offspring would be afflicted for 400 _____.
6 Abraham was _____ to keep the way of the LORD.
8 Ishmael was the son of Abram and _____.
10 God promised to make Abram into a great _____.

Genesis 19–26

Answer in complete sentences.

1. Why did God destroy Sodom and Gomorrah?

2. Why did Hagar and Ishmael leave Abraham?

3. What did God command Abraham to do to Isaac?

4. Why did Abraham call the mount of the LORD, "The LORD will provide"?

5. What did Abraham ask his servant to do for Isaac?

6. Why did Isaac pray to the LORD about his wife?

7. For what did Esau sell his birthright?

8. What did God promise Isaac?

_____

_____

Jacob (Genesis 27–35)

Directions: Circle the letter of the best answer.

1. Who told Jacob to get Esau's blessing?
   (a) Sarah
   (b) Rebekah
   (c) Dinah
   (d) Rachel

2. How did Jacob convince Isaac he was Esau?
   (a) He took a Canaanite wife.
   (b) He hunted like Esau.
   (c) He put red clothing on.
   (d) He wore skins and Esau's clothes.

3. After he was deceived, what did Esau plan to do to Jacob?
   (a) Murder Jacob
   (b) Pray for Jacob
   (c) Strike Jacob
   (d) Bless Jacob

4. Who told Jacob to find a wife in Paddan-aram?
   (a) Esau
   (b) Abraham
   (c) Rebekah
   (d) Isaac

5. What were the angels doing in Jacob's dream?
   (a) Feeding him
   (b) Flying to and fro
   (c) Ascending and descending on a ladder
   (d) Praying for the lost

6. How many years did Jacob work for Rachel?
   (a) 5
   (b) 7
   (c) 9
   (d) 11

7. How did Laban deceive Jacob?
   (a) He gave Jacob Leah instead of Rachel.
   (b) He hid his daughters.
   (c) He gave his daughter to another man.
   (d) He gave Jacob Rachel instead of Leah.

8. Which wife bore Jacob's first four sons?
   (a) Leah
   (b) Rachel
   (c) Bilhah
   (d) Zilpah

9. Why did Rachel give Bilhah to Jacob as a wife?
   (a) Rachel disliked Jacob.
   (b) Rachel disliked Bilhah.
   (c) Rachel was barren.
   (d) Rachel loved Bilhah.

10. When Jacob returned from Paddan-aram, why was he afraid of Esau?

    (a) Esau was coming with 400 men to meet Jacob.

    (b) Esau was a great sword-fighter.

    (c) Esau wanted vengeance.

    (d) Esau was a king.

11. When Jacob returned from Paddan-aram, how did he plan to please Esau?

    (a) by avoiding him

    (b) by promising him goodwill

    (c) by sending presents ahead of him

    (d) by bringing his father

12. Jacob wrestled with a man. Why did the man change Jacob's name to Israel?

    (a) The land should be named after him.

    (b) The man didn't like the name "Jacob."

    (c) The man loved Jacob.

    (d) Jacob struggled with God and man, and he prevailed.

13. When Jacob returned from Paddan-aram, how did Esau treat Jacob?

    (a) He hugged and kissed him.

    (b) He bruised and beat him.

    (c) He gave him many presents.

    (d) He demanded his blessing.

14. What did Shechem, the son of Hamor, do to Dinah?

    (a) He lay with her when they were unmarried.

    (b) He gave her a beautiful diamond.

    (c) He murdered her.

    (d) He sang songs to her.

15. How did Simeon and Levi avenge the wrong done to Dinah?

    (a) They demanded money from those in Shechem.

    (b) They murdered those in Shechem.

    (c) They imprisoned those in Shechem.

    (d) They burned the town of Shechem.

16. God commanded Jacob to go to Bethel. What did Jacob command his family?

    (a) Pray to the LORD.

    (b) Give to the poor.

    (c) Get rid of your gods and purify yourselves.

    (d) Be kind to one another.

17. What happened to Rachel after she gave birth to Benjamin?

    (a) She gave birth to two more children.

    (b) She returned to Paddan-aram.

    (c) She mourned for Joseph.

    (d) She died.

Genesis 37–41

Hint: Words are only found forward: down, right or diagonal.

```
I  M  Y  E  U  B  G  Q  C  D  P  V
R  N  R  M  G  N  L  X  O  T  O  B
E  Z  T  K  H  O  V  E  W  X  Q  T
M  X  J  E  A  L  O  U  S  Y  T  C
E  W  N  I  R  I  H  I  G  S  B  S
M  D  I  Q  W  P  D  E  U  W  E  U
B  K  N  S  H  S  R  Z  W  B  A  D
E  O  F  P  D  P  E  E  H  O  B  C
R  D  O  A  C  O  A  L  T  M  Q  S
E  P  H  R  A  I  M  L  I  E  M  D
M  Q  E  S  S  I  I  N  L  W  D  U
```

1. Joseph's brothers' sheaves bowed to him in his __ __ __ __ __ __.

2. Jacob's sons felt hatred and __ __ __ __ __ __ __ __ towards Joseph.

3. God __ __ __ __ __ __ __ Potiphar's household while Joseph was there.

4. Potiphar's wife accused Joseph of trying to __ __ __ with her.

5. Joseph __ __ __ __ __ __ __ __ __ __ __ the chief cupbearer's and chief baker's dreams.

6. Joseph asked the chief cupbearer to __ __ __ __ __ __ __ __ him.

7. Pharaoh dreamed about __ __ __ __ __ and grain.

8. Pharaoh chose Joseph as second-in-command because of his __ __ __ __ __ __ __.

147

9. Joseph's sons were Manasseh and _ _ _ _ _ _ _.

Genesis 42–50

Directions: Fill in the blanks.

1. During his brothers' first visit, Joseph treated them as _____.

2. The _____ was severe, so Joseph's brothers returned to Egypt.

3. _____ came with his brothers on the second trip.

4. The _____ cup was found in Benjamin's sack.

5. _____ offered to be Joseph's servant.

6. _____ moved to Egypt to see Joseph and survive the famine.

7. _____ people belonging to Jacob came to Egypt.

8. Jacob took Manasseh and Ephraim as _____.

9. Jacob put his _____ hand on Ephraim's head.

10. The _____ shall not depart from Judah.

11. Jacob commanded his sons to _____ him in Canaan.

12. Joseph's _____ feared Joseph would repay them the evil done to him.

Exodus 1–4

In one paragraph, describe God's first meeting with Moses. Use at least 6 sentences. Do not forget: (1) how God appeared; (2) what Moses was doing; (3) why God was concerned; (4) God's name; and (5) Moses' reservations.

_____

_____

_____

_____

_____

_____

_____

_____

_____

_____

_____

_____

_____

_____

_____

_____

Exodus 7–12

Write the Ten Plagues, in order.

Plague 1 _____

Plague 2 _____

Plague 3 _____

Plague 4 _____

Plague 5 _____

Plague 6 _____

Plague 7 _____

Plague 8 _____

Plague 9 _____

Plague 10 _____

Exodus 13–18

Answer in complete sentences.

1. Why were the firstborn set aside for God?

2. In what form did God lead the Israelites out of Egypt?

3. How did God save the Israelites near the Red Sea?

4. What did Moses and the Israelites do after God saved them from the Egyptians at the Red Sea?

5. What was wrong with the water at Marah?

6. What food did God provide the Israelites for 40 years?

7. What happened at Massah and Meribah?

8. What did Amalek do to Israel?

   _____

   _____

9. How did Jethro advise Moses?

   _____

   _____

Sinai (Exodus 19–31)

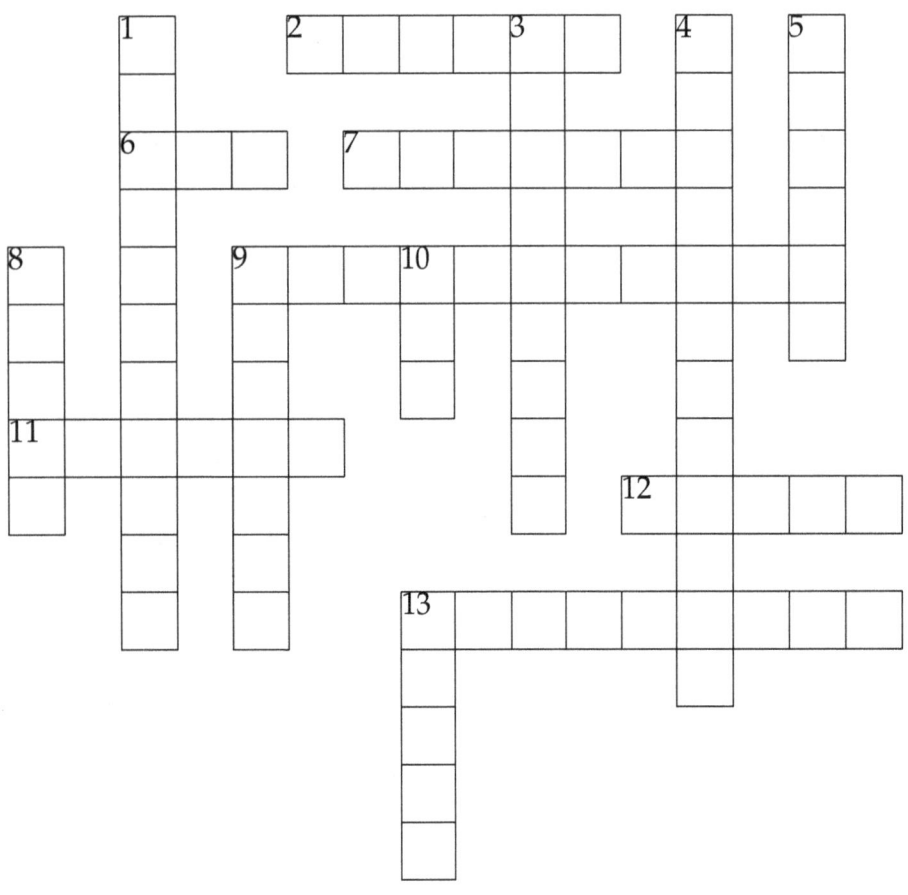

Across

2 Treat sojourners _____.
6 Moses and other leaders saw _____.
7 If Israel kept God's law God promised to make them a _____ of priests.
9 The _____ had 12 stones on it.
11 The priest wore a _____ around his head.
12 God spoke to Moses from the _____ seat.
13 The table for bread _____ and incense altar went in the Holy Place.

Down

1 Keep the feasts of unleavened bread harvest and _____.
3 God came upon Mount Sinai in thunder and _____.
4 God first gave the Ten _____ from Mount Sinai.
5 "All the LORD has _____ we will do."
8 Moses spent _____ days and nights on Mount Sinai.
9 God appointed _____ and Oholiab to build the worship things.
10 The _____ of the covenant went in the Most Holy Place.
13 Two _____ were sacrificed daily.

The Tabernacle (Exodus 32–40)

Directions: Circle the letter of the best answer.

1. As Moses delayed coming from the mountain, what did the people ask Aaron to do?

    (a) Sing praises

    (b) Offer sacrifices

    (c) Build gods

    (d) Leave Moses

2. After the people worshipped the golden calf, what did God plan to do?

    (a) Destroy them

    (b) Leave them

    (c) Take the law from them

    (d) Cease loving them

3. When Moses saw the calf and the people dancing, what did he do with the tablets?

    (a) Read them

    (b) Smashed them

    (c) Displayed them

    (d) Wrote on them

4. Which tribe was on Moses' and the LORD's side?

    (a) Judah

    (b) Naphtali

    (c) Gad

    (d) Levi

5. What would the people do as Moses went to the Tent of Meeting?

    (a) Stand and worship

    (b) Their daily business

    (c) Prepare for battle

    (d) Sacrifice

6. What special thing did Moses see?

    (a) His children

    (b) The land of Canaan

    (c) The tabernacle

    (d) God's back in all his glory

7. When Moses went to Sinai the second time, God declared he is . . .

    (a) strong and mighty

    (b) merciful and gracious

    (c) everlasting and all-knowing

    (d) holy and righteous

8. Why did Moses put a veil over his face?

    (a) He looked bad.

    (b) His eyes had trouble with light.

    (c) He didn't want to see others.

    (d) His face shone after talking with God.

9. Who in Israel contributed goods for building the tabernacle and its furnishings?

   (a) Everyone

   (b) The rich

   (c) Those with generous hearts

   (d) The priests

10. Why did Moses ask the people to quit contributing?

    (a) They gave plenty.

    (b) Moses decided not to build the tabernacle.

    (c) God contributed the rest.

    (d) They didn't give cheerfully.

11. How well did the people obey God in constructing the tabernacle?

    (a) Not at all

    (b) Poorly

    (c) Okay

    (d) Very well

12. Why couldn't Moses enter the tent of meeting?

    (a) It wasn't constructed.

    (b) Only Aaron was allowed inside.

    (c) The glory of the LORD filled the tabernacle.

    (d) He was unclean.

Leviticus 1–16

Answer in complete sentences.

1. What were the five offerings?

2. What did the sin offering do?

3. What did the LORD do to Aaron's first burnt offering?

4. Nadab and Abihu offered unauthorized fire before the LORD. What happened to them?

5. What happened on the Day of Atonement (for the people and all Israel)?

6. What was special about the goat for Azazel?

Leviticus 17–26

In one paragraph, describe the Year of Jubilee.

In one paragraph, describe what God would do if Israel obeyed his commands, and what God would do if Israel disobeyed his commands. Do not forget the chance to return to him.

Numbers 1–12

Directions: Circle the letter of the best answer.

1. Which tribe had the most men?
   (a) Reuben
   (b) Simeon
   (c) Levi
   (d) Judah

2. Which tribe took care of the tabernacle?
   (a) Dan
   (b) Gad
   (c) Levi
   (d) Judah

3. Who substituted for the firstborn?
   (a) Levi
   (b) Ephraim
   (c) Benjamin
   (d) Naphtali

4. What are the three special rules of a Nazirite?
   (a) pray daily, do not cut hair, avoid alcohol
   (b) do not cut hair, avoid alcohol, avoid dead bodies
   (c) pray daily, avoid dead bodies, obey the Sabbath
   (d) avoid alcohol, obey the Sabbath, practice kindness

5. Why does someone become a Nazirite?
   (a) to be honored
   (b) to become king
   (c) to separate themselves to God
   (d) to become priest

6. What did the chiefs offer for each tribe?
   (a) a silver plate
   (b) a gold dish
   (c) a bull
   (d) all of the above

7. Who determined when Israel set out and when they remained?
   (a) Moses
   (b) Joshua
   (c) Caleb
   (d) God

8. What was the purpose of the two silver trumpets?
   (a) to summon Israel
   (b) to honor God
   (c) to decorate the tabernacle
   (d) to announce meal times

9. What did Moses ask Hobab?
   (a) to heal his mother
   (b) to find water
   (c) to remain with them
   (d) to build an altar

10. How did God help Moses govern all the people?

   (a) He gave Moses more of His Spirit.
   (b) He put some of Moses' spirit on 70 elders.
   (c) He made Joshua co-judge.
   (d) He gave Moses a break.

11. The people craved meat. What did God do?

   (a) He ignored them.
   (b) He sent cattle from Egypt.
   (c) He rained fish from heaven.
   (d) He blew in quail from the sea.

12. Why should Miriam and Aaron fear to speak against Moses?

   (a) God spoke with Moses face to face.
   (b) God chose Moses.
   (c) Moses was strong.
   (d) Moses used to be an Egyptian.

Numbers 13–21

Directions: Fill in the blanks.

1. Moses sent spies to Canaan to check out the _____ and its people.

2. The spies returned and reported that the land was great but the people were _____.

3. Two spies, _____ and _____, warned the people not to rebel but to trust God.

4. Because the people rebelled, God made them remain in the desert _____ years.

5. The _____ opened and swallowed all who belonged to Korah.

6. The LORD gave every _____ in Israel to the Levites for an inheritance.

7. _____ and _____ did not uphold the LORD as holy at Meribah; therefore, they could not enter the promised land.

8. Those bitten by _____ could look at a bronze _____ and live.

Numbers 22–30

Hint: Words are only found forward or down.

```
G H H X B L C C M Y R C D
V F T Q L Y V F P X M G D
Y S A H E J O S H U A H A
N P R L S G W F I W A D S
W O R D S U G A N G E L R
Q K Z M E C A L E B P G S
Z E X P D A U G H T E R S
W Z A D U Z O C A K G L Q
F R X H E Z O H S S L Q K
```

1. Balaam's donkey saved him from an __ __ __ __ __.

2. Balaam's donkey __ __ __ __ __ to Balaam.

3. God wanted Balaam to speak only the __ __ __ __ __ God spoke.

4. Instead of cursing Israel, Balaam __ __ __ __ __ __ __ Israel.

5. __ __ __ __ __ __ __ __ turned back God's wrath by killing an Israelite and a Midianite woman.

6. Joshua and __ __ __ __ __ were the only survivors from the first census.

7. If a man had no son, his inheritance passed first to his __ __ __ __ __ __ __ __ __.

8. God appointed __ __ __ __ __ __ to succeed Moses.

9. If a man made a __ __ __ __ to the LORD, he must keep it.

162

Numbers 31–35

Answer in complete sentences.

1. Why did God want vengeance on Midian?

2. How many Israelites died in the battle with Midian?

3. Where did Reuben, Gad and half of Manasseh want to settle?

4. What must Reuben, Gad and half of Manasseh do in order to settle there?

5. How were the Israelites to divide the land?

6. How many cities would the Levites inherit?

7. What happened to someone who accidentally murdered another?

Deuteronomy 1–6

Deuteronomy 1–6 mentions the word "love." In one paragraph, explain how "love" is used.

Moses tells the Israelites, "These words that I command you today shall be on your heart." In one paragraph, describe the ways Moses recommends to put God's law on their hearts.

Deuteronomy 7–12

Directions: Circle the letter of the best answer.

1. How should Israel relate with the Canaanites?

    (a) They should try to get along.

    (b) They should destroy them.

    (c) They should borrow their things.

    (d) They should greet them kindly.

2. Why did God let the people go hungry and provide them with manna?

    (a) He forgot about their needs.

    (b) He wanted them to provide for themselves.

    (c) He wanted to show them a miracle.

    (d) He wanted to teach them that man does not live on bread alone, but by every word that comes from God.

3. What is not a reason God gave the Israelites the land?

    (a) The Canaanites were wicked.

    (b) God loved Israel.

    (c) God chose Israel to be holy.

    (d) Israel was righteous.

4. What was wrong with Israel's righteousness?

    (a) They were stubborn.

    (b) They did not sacrifice enough.

    (c) They loved God too much.

    (d) They hated evil.

5. What did God command Israel to do with their hearts?

    (a) Circumcise them.

    (b) Feed them.

    (c) Open them.

    (d) Exercise them.

6. How should Israel treat sojourners?

    (a) Hate them.

    (b) Ignore them.

    (c) Love them.

    (d) Enslave them.

7. What is the blessing and curse Moses set before Israel?

    (a) bless for loving; curse for not loving

    (b) bless for studying; curse for not studying

    (c) bless for sacrificing; curse for not sacrificing

    (d) bless for obedience; curse for disobedience

8. If Israel was careful to obey, what would God do to the Canaanites?

    (a) Bless them.

    (b) Drive them out.

    (c) Kill them.

    (d) Join them to Israel.

9. Where should Israel offer sacrifices in the land?

   (a) in the one place God chooses

   (b) any place they build an altar

   (c) Mount Ebal

   (d) Beersheba

Deuteronomy 14–20

Directions: Fill in the blanks.

1. Clean animals have a _____ hoof and chew the _____.

2. Clean sea animals have _____ and _____.

3. From their crops, Israel should give God a _____.

4. Loans to the poor should be released every _____ years.

5. Judges shall follow _____, and only _____.

6. Charges in court cases must be established by _____ or more witnesses.

7. The LORD will raise up a _____ after Moses to speak God's words.

8. Israel should not _____ battles against larger armies, because the LORD fights for Israel.

Deuteronomy 21–28

Why should a child not be put to death for a father's sin? Answer in a complete sentence.

_____

_____

_____

From which two mountains would the Israelites declare the blessings for obedience and the curses for disobedience? Answer in one or two complete sentences.

_____

_____

_____

Make two lists. List at least four things under each list. The list titles are below.

Blessings for Obedience	Curses for Disobedience
_____	_____
_____	_____
_____	_____
_____	_____

Deuteronomy 29–34

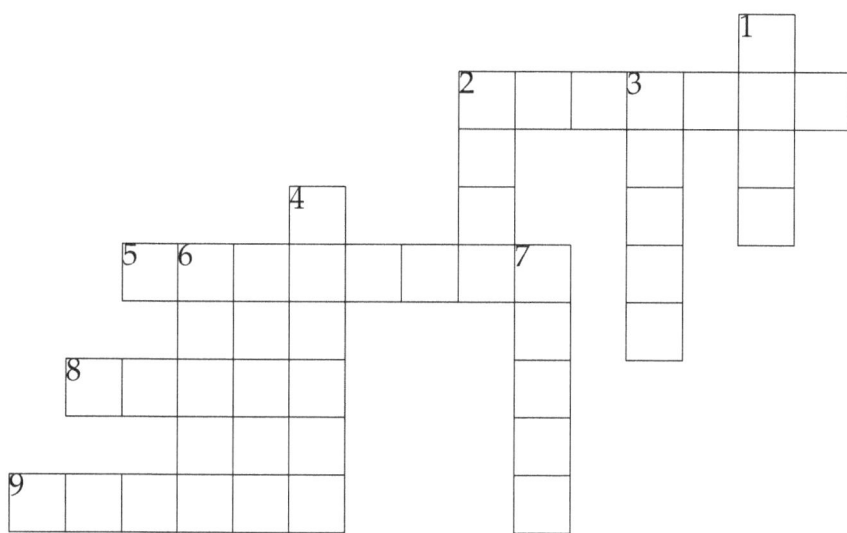

Across
2 In Moses' song, after they were blessed, Israel _____ God.
5 _____ things belong to us and our children.
8 When he died, Moses' _____ was unabated.
9 After God's curse there was hope if Israel would _____.

Down
1 God predicted Israel would go after other _____.
2 The LORD knew Moses face to _____.
3 Israel publicly read the law every _____ years.
4 _____ things belong to God.
6 In Moses' song God is like an _____.
7 I lay before you life and _____.

Joshua 1–6

Hint: Words are only found forward: down, right or diagonal.

```
U X V F M T S J C H U C R
Z M L E F D D T I O T O I
A A O D Q U R L R C E R L
H N I D Z G T C C O F D C
S N U B J M W A U R N O Y
P A S S O V E R M R X G I
J V A P R Y L D C P S M B
Z F H I D F V D I J A E K
Y R A H A B E J S T F V X
S R S Y N A M J E D A P T
D Z W A A R V A S T A T A
Q S H O U T L C R C Y E E
```

1. _ _ _ _ _ _ _ _ on the Law day and night.

2. Be _ _ _ _ _ _ _ and courageous.

3. Rahab _ _ _ the spies on her roof.

4. _ _ _ _ _ said, "The LORD is God in the heavens and earth."

5. Israel would spare Rahab and her family if she tied a scarlet _ _ _ _ in her window.

6. When the priests carrying the ark stepped in the _ _ _ _ _ _, the water rose in a heap.

7. Israel gathered _ _ _ _ _ _ _ stones from the Jordan.

8. Joshua paused before Jericho to _ _ _ _ _ _ _ _ _ _ Israel.

9. On the fourteenth day of the first month, Israel celebrated _ _ _ _ _ _ _ _.

10. On that day, the _ _ _ _ _ ceased.

11. When the people heard the trumpet, they gave a great _ _ _ _ _ and the wall fell down flat.

12. Joshua laid a _ _ _ _ _ on whoever rebuilt Jericho.

Joshua 7–13

Answer in complete sentences.

1. What did Achan do wrong?

2. What happened to Israel because Achan sinned?

3. After the battle of Ai, what did Israel do from Mount Ebal and Mount Gerizim?

4. How did the Gibeonites make peace with Israel?

5. How were the Gibeonites punished?

6. Why did Joshua march all night to help Gibeon?

7. Name two ways God helped Israel in the battle of Gibeon.

8. Why didn't more cities make peace with Israel?

_____

_____

Joshua 14–24

Directions: Circle the letter of the best answer.

1. Which city did the LORD give Caleb?

    (a) Hebron

    (b) Beersheba

    (c) Jerusalem

    (d) Jericho

2. How many tribes were slow to take their portion of the land?

    (a) 3

    (b) 5

    (c) 7

    (d) 9

3. How many of God's promises to Israel about the land failed?

    (a) 0

    (b) 1

    (c) 2

    (d) 3

4. The transjordan tribes built an altar. What did the western tribes think of it?

    (a) They liked it.

    (b) They didn't care about it.

    (c) They coveted it.

    (d) They prepared for war.

5. Why did the transjordan tribes build the altar?

    (a) It was a memorial that the LORD was their God, too.

    (b) It was used for sacrifice to the LORD.

    (c) It was used for sacrifice to false gods.

    (d) It was a memorial that God gave them the land.

6. God brought the good things he promised for Israel. In the same way,

    (a) God would bring more good things in the future.

    (b) God would bring bad things on them if they disobeyed.

    (c) God would bring good things upon all people.

    (d) God would bring bad things on their enemies.

7. What choice did Joshua give Israel?

    (a) Which god will you serve?

    (b) What land do you want?

    (c) What day will be the Sabbath?

    (d) Who will lead after me?

8. What served as a witness over that choice?

    (a) an altar

    (b) a mountain

    (c) a temple

    (d) a stone

Judges 1–5

Describe the Judges Cycle. Include all the steps.

Tell the story of Deborah, Barak, Sisera and Jael. Include all the major events. Use at least four sentences.

Judges 6–11

Across

2 Abimelech was badly wounded by a ____.

4 Fire sprang from the rock, and the ____ vanished.

7 He vowed to sacrifice whatever came from his ____.

8 Jotham placed a ____ on Abimelech and Shechem.

10 ____ was driven from his home, because of his mother.

Down

1 Israel asked Gideon to be ____, but Gideon refused.

3 Gideon used torches, jars and ____ to defeat Midian.

4 Gideon asked those who were ____ to go home.

5 Gideon made a golden ____ with the war spoils.

6 Gideon's other name.

9 Gideon pursued ____ and Zalmunna east of the Jordan.

Judges 13–21

Directions: Fill in the blanks.

1. The _____ told Manoah's wife she would have a son.

2. Samson was a _____ from birth.

3. Samson wanted to marry a _____.

4. "Out of the _____ came something to eat. Out of the _____ came something sweet."

5. When Samson heard his wife was given to someone else, he _____ the grain fields of the Philistines.

6. The Spirit of the Lord rushed on Samson, and he struck 1,000 men with a donkey's _____.

7. After the battle, God gave Samson _____.

8. _____ discovered the secret of Samson's strength.

9. She had Samson's _____ cut, and he became like any other man.

10. Samson asked God for strength one last time, and he toppled the _____ of Dagon upon himself and the Philistines.

11. Micah's mother made an _____.

12. The _____ stole Micah's idol and priest.

13. The men of _____ terribly treated a Levite's concubine.

14. Benjamin defeated Israel _____ times before Israel defeated them.

15. After Benjamin's defeat, Israel helped them get _____.

Ruth 1–4

Directions: Circle the letter of the best answer.

1. What did Naomi lose in Moab?

    (a) her land

    (b) her faith

    (c) her husband and sons

    (d) her house

2. Naomi returned to Israel. What was Ruth determined to do?

    (a) stay with Naomi

    (b) remain in Moab

    (c) return to her Moabite gods

    (d) find a new husband

3. In whose field did Ruth glean?

    (a) David's

    (b) Elimelech's

    (c) Obed's

    (d) Boaz's

4. How did Boaz treat Ruth?

    (a) indifferently

    (b) kindly

    (c) cruelly

    (d) adoringly

5. Boaz ate, drank and lay down. What did Ruth do that night?

    (a) She stayed with Naomi.

    (b) She returned to Moab.

    (c) She cried for Boaz.

    (d) She lay at Boaz's feet.

6. Ruth asked Boaz to cover her with his wings. What did Boaz promise?

    (a) to see if the nearest redeemer wanted her

    (b) to find good wings for her

    (c) to marry Ruth

    (d) to restore Elimelech's land

7. Boaz purchased Naomi's property. Who witnessed it?

    (a) Naomi and Ruth

    (b) his friends

    (c) Samson

    (d) the elders of Bethlehem

8. What was the name of Boaz's and Ruth's son?

    (a) Obed

    (b) Mahlon

    (c) Elimelech

    (d) David

Part IV

Year Two
(1 Samuel through Nehemiah, Jeremiah, Daniel)

10 Year Two Plan

1. 1 Samuel 1   *Memorize* 1 Samuel 2:1–8

   (a) Why was Hannah sad?

   (b) What did Hannah pray?

2. 1 Samuel 2

   (a) Name some sins of Eli's sons.

   (b) What did the man of God predict about Eli's family?

3. 1 Samuel 3

   (a) When the LORD first called Samuel, who did Samuel think called him?

   (b) What did the LORD tell Samuel?

4. 1 Samuel 4

   (a) What did the Israelites believe would give them victory over Philistia?

   (b) What happened to Eli and his sons?

5. 1 Samuel 5–6

   (a) What happened to the Philistines when they had the ark?

   (b) How did the Philistines know the plagues were from God?

6. 1 Samuel 7–8

   (a) If the people truly wanted to return to the LORD, what did Samuel advise?

   (b) The Israelites repented at Mizpah. What did the Philistines do?

   (c) What was wrong with Samuel's sons?

   (d) What did the Israelites request?

7. 1 Samuel 9:1—10:16

   (a) How did Saul happen to meet Samuel?

   (b) What happened to Saul as he came to Gibeah?

8. 1 Samuel 10:17—11:15

   (a) At Mizpah, Saul was chosen by lot to be king. Where was Saul?

   (b) When Saul heard of the plight of Jabesh-gilead, what did he do?

9. 1 Samuel 12   <u>Test</u>: 1 Samuel 1–8

(a) Samuel assembled the people and their king at Gilgal. What sin did he confront them with?

(b) Samuel asked God to show that asking for a king was wicked. What did he ask him to do?

10. 1 Samuel 13

    (a) Why would Saul's kingdom not continue?

    (b) The Philistines camped at Michmash; how hard-pressed was Israel?

11. 1 Samuel 14:1–46

    (a) How did God work through Jonathan and his armor-bearer?

    (b) What vow did Saul make that harmed the army?

12. 1 Samuel 14:47—15:35

    (a) How did Saul disobey God's command about the Amalekites?

    (b) Complete the sentence: "Because you have rejected the word of the LORD ..."

13. 1 Samuel 16

    (a) Whom did Samuel anoint king after Saul?

    (b) How was Saul refreshed when the evil spirit tormented him?

14. 1 Samuel 17   <u>Test</u>: 1 Samuel 9–15

    (a) Why did David visit his brothers in the army?

    (b) What challenge did Goliath give Israel's army?

    (c) Why was David confident he could beat Goliath?

    (d) How did David defeat Goliath?

15. 1 Samuel 18

    (a) Name some ways David grew in popularity and power.

    (b) How did Saul feel about David's popularity?

16. 1 Samuel 19

    (a) Saul planned to kill David (the first time). What did Jonathan do?

    (b) David was with Samuel. What happened to Saul when he came to get him?

17. 1 Samuel 20

    (a) How did Jonathan discover that Saul meant to harm David?

    (b) How did Jonathan inform David of his discovery?

18. 1 Samuel 21–22   *Memorize* 2 Samuel 1:19–27

    (a) How did Ahimelech help David?

    (b) What happened to Ahimelech at Nob?

19. 1 Samuel 23

    (a) What was Keilah's problem and how was it fixed?

20. 1 Samuel 24   <u>Test</u>: 1 Samuel 16–20

    (a) Saul went into the cave near Engedi to relieve himself. What did David do?

    (b) Why wouldn't David harm Saul?

21. 1 Samuel 25

    (a) How did Nabal treat David's men?

    (b) What did Abigail do about her husband's actions?

    (c) What did David plan, and why did he change his mind?

22. 1 Samuel 26–27

    (a) What did David do when Saul encamped on the hill of Hachilah?

    (b) After David spared Saul near Hachilah, where did David go?

23. 1 Samuel 28–29

    (a) The Philistines gathered at Aphek. Whom did Saul consult for help?

    (b) Why did Achish send David away?

24. 1 Samuel 30

    (a) When David returned from Aphek, what was wrong with Ziklag?

    (b) What rule did David make about those in the battle and those with the baggage?

25. 1 Samuel 31—2 Samuel 1

    (a) How did Saul die?

    (b) What happened to the Amalekite who claimed he killed Saul?

26. 2 Samuel 2

    (a) When David moved from Ziklag, where did he go?

    (b) How did Asahel die?

27. 2 Samuel 3   <u>Test</u>: 1 Samuel 21—2 Samuel 1

(a) Why did Abner plan to give the throne to David?

(b) Joab murdered Abner. How did David respond?

28. 2 Samuel 4:1—5:16

    (a) How did Ish-bosheth die?

    (b) David moved from Hebron to where?

29. 2 Samuel 5:17—6:23

    (a) How did Uzzah die?

    (b) Why was Michal angry with David?

30. 2 Samuel 7

    (a) After the LORD had given him rest from his enemies, what troubled David?

    (b) What did God promise David?

31. 2 Samuel 8–9

    (a) Why was David victorious wherever he went?

    (b) How did David show Saul's house kindness?

32. 2 Samuel 10

    (a) How did Joab defeat the Ammonites?

33. 2 Samuel 11

    (a) What sin did David commit with Bathsheba?

    (b) How did David try to cover up his sin with Bathsheba?

34. 2 Samuel 12   <u>Test</u>: 2 Samuel 2–10

    (a) What story did Nathan tell David?

    (b) What was David's punishment for his adultery and murder?

35. 2 Samuel 13

    (a) Why did Absalom hate Amnon and murder him?

    (b) Where did Absalom flee after he murdered Amnon?

36. 2 Samuel 14

    (a) Why did David bring Absalom back from Geshur?

37. 2 Samuel 15

    (a) How did Absalom steal the hearts of the men of Israel?

(b) When David heard of Absalom's conspiracy, what did he do?

38. 2 Samuel 16–17

   (a) What did Shimei do as David fled Jerusalem?

   (b) How did Ahithophel's advice and Hushai's advice differ?

39. 2 Samuel 18:1—19:8 *Memorize* 2 Samuel 23:13–17

   (a) What orders did David give his army concerning Absalom?

   (b) How did Absalom die?

40. 2 Samuel 19:9–43

   (a) Which tribe of Israel brought David back as king after Absalom's death?

41. 2 Samuel 20:1—21:14

   (a) Why didn't Amasa become commander of David's army?

   (b) Why did God cause a three-year famine during David's reign?

42. 2 Samuel 21:15—22:51 Test: 2 Samuel 11–19

   (a) Who saved David from Ishbi-benob?

   (b) What did David write when the LORD delivered him from his enemies?

43. 2 Samuel 23

   (a) How many mighty men did David have?

44. 2 Samuel 24

   (a) Why did God punish Israel, giving David three options?

   (b) Where did the plague stop?

45. 1 Kings 1

   (a) Who plotted to become king after David?

   (b) Who spoke to David about Adonijah's plot?

46. 1 Kings 2 Test: 2 Samuel 19–24

   (a) What did David command Solomon about the law before he died?

   (b) What men did Solomon deal with to firmly establish his kingdom?

47. 1 Kings 3

   (a) What did Solomon request?

   (b) How did Solomon show wisdom before the two prostitutes?

48. 1 Kings 4   *Memorize* 1 Kings 3:10–14

    (a) Why did people from all nations come to see Solomon?

49. 1 Kings 5–6

    (a) With whom did Solomon make a treaty?

    (b) How many years did it take Solomon to complete the temple?

50. 1 Kings 7

    (a) Besides the temple, what other structure did Solomon build?

    (b) What skillful worker from Tyre helped with the temple furnishings?

51. 1 Kings 8:1–30

    (a) What filled the temple after the ark was put in it?

    (b) Solomon stood before the altar in front of the people of Israel and did what?

52. 1 Kings 8:31–66

    (a) In Solomon's prayer, what problem of the people does he speak about?

    (b) How did the people feel after the temple's dedication?

53. 1 Kings 9

    (a) On what condition would God establish Solomon's throne forever?

54. 1 Kings 10   <u>Test</u>: 1 Kings 1–8

    (a) What queen came to hear Solomon's wisdom?

    (b) Give some evidence that Solomon was rich.

55. 1 Kings 11

    (a) What did Solomon do wrong?

    (b) How did God punish Solomon for his sin?

56. 1 Kings 12

    (a) Why did Israel rebel against Rehoboam?

    (b) Jeroboam worried people would sacrifice in Jerusalem. What did he do?

57. 1 Kings 13

    (a) What did the man of God prophesy about Jeroboam's altar?

    (b) Why did the man of God die on his way home?

58. 1 Kings 14

(a) What did Ahijah prophesy about Israel's future?

(b) What did Shishak, king of Egypt, do to Jerusalem?

59. 2 Chronicles 11–12

(a) What book parallels 1 and 2 Kings?

60. 1 Kings 15:1–8, 2 Chronicles 13

(a) With whom did Abijah fight a great battle?

61. 1 Kings 15:9–24, 2 Chronicles 14–16

(a) Name some good things Asa did.

(b) Why was God angry with Asa?

62. 1 Kings 15:25—16:34

(a) Who destroyed Jeroboam's family?

(b) How evil was Ahab, compared to other kings?

63. 1 Kings 17

(a) What did Elijah tell Ahab the first time they met?

(b) How did God provide for Elijah during the drought?

64. 1 Kings 18   <u>Test</u>: 1 Kings 9–16

(a) When Elijah met Ahab, what did he command?

(b) Describe the contest between Baal and God.

65. 1 Kings 19   *Memorize* 1 Kings 18:36–39

(a) Jezebel threatened to kill Elijah. What did Elijah do?

(b) How did God appear to Elijah at Horeb?

(c) What tasks did God give Elijah at Horeb?

66. 1 Kings 20

(a) Ahab defeated Ben-hadad. What did Ahab do wrong?

67. 1 Kings 21

(a) How did Ahab get Naboth's vineyard?

(b) How did God punish Ahab for his dealings with Naboth?

68. 1 Kings 22:1–40

(a) Whom did Ahab ask to fight with him for Ramoth-gilead?

(b) What did Micaiah say was wrong with the other prophets?

69. 2 Chronicles 17, 19

(a) Name some good things Jehoshaphat did.

(b) What did God think about Jehoshaphat's alliance with Ahab?

70. 2 Chronicles 20 <u>Test</u>: 1 Kings 17–22

(a) When Jehoshaphat heard of a great army against him, what did he do?

(b) How did God deliver Judah?

71. 2 Kings 1

(a) Why did Ahaziah, son of Ahab, die?

(b) What happened when a captain and fifty men came to seize Elijah?

72. 2 Chronicles 21

(a) How did Jehoram, Jehoshaphat's son, behave?

(b) How did God punish Jehoram?

73. 2 Kings 2

(a) Did Elijah die? What happened?

(b) How did the prophets of Jericho know that the spirit of Elijah rested on Elisha?

74. 2 Kings 3 *Memorize* 2 Kings 6:15–17

(a) How did God help the armies of Israel, Judah and Edom?

75. 2 Kings 4 <u>Test</u>: 2 Chronicles 17–21, 2 Kings 1–2

(a) What things did Elisha do for the wealthy woman in Shunem?

76. 2 Kings 5

(a) What miracle happened to Naaman?

(b) Why did Gehazi get Naaman's leprosy?

77. 2 Kings 6:1–23

(a) How were the king of Syria's movements known to the king of Israel?

(b) Why did Elisha say, "Do not be afraid," when an army surrounded his city?

78. 2 Kings 6:24—7:20

(a) When the king of Israel heard how a woman boiled her son, what did he plan?

(b) Who discovered that the Syrians had fled?

79. 2 Kings 8

   (a) How did Hazael become king of Syria?

80. 2 Kings 9

   (a) What did Elisha do to Jehu?

   (b) How did Jehu become king?

81. 2 Kings 10 Test: 2 Kings 3–7

   (a) How did Jehu put an end to Baal worship?

   (b) Jehu mostly followed the LORD. How did he still mess up?

82. 2 Chronicles 22:10—23:21

   (a) After Ahaziah died, who took the throne of Judah?

   (b) How did Joash gain the throne?

83. 2 Chronicles 24

   (a) What great thing did Joash do?

   (b) What terrible thing did Joash do?

84. 2 Kings 13 *Memorize* 2 Kings 17:13–18

   (a) What happened to a dead man when his body was thrown on Elisha's bones?

85. 2 Chronicles 25

   (a) What did Amaziah do with Edom's gods?

86. 2 Chronicles 26 Test: 2 Kings 8–13, 2 Chronicles 22–24

   (a) What did Uzziah do in the days of Zechariah?

   (b) Why did God strike Uzziah with leprosy?

87. 2 Kings 14:23—15:31

   (a) Which nation began to trouble Israel during the reign of Menahem?

88. 2 Kings 15:32—16:20

   (a) When Rezin and Pekah came against Judah, whom did Ahaz ask for help?

   (b) Name some evil things Ahaz did.

89. 2 Kings 17

   (a) Why was Israel conquered and exiled?

(b) Which god did the Samaritans serve?

90. 2 Kings 18

    (a) What kind of king was Hezekiah?
    (b) What did the Rabshakeh of Assyria declare about the LORD?

91. 2 Kings 19

    (a) Which prophet reassured Hezekiah?
    (b) How were the Assyrians forced to leave?

92. 2 Kings 20

    (a) What sign did God work to show Hezekiah he would live longer?
    (b) What did Isaiah say Babylon would do?

93. 2 Kings 21

    (a) How evil was Manasseh?
    (b) What did the prophets prophesy about Judah because of Manasseh's sin?

94. 2 Kings 22 Test: 2 Kings 14–20

    (a) What did Hilkiah find?
    (b) Why did Josiah tear his robes?

95. 2 Kings 23:1–30

    (a) What good things did Josiah do?
    (b) How did Josiah die?

96. 2 Kings 23:31—24:17

    (a) Judah was captured during which king's reign?
    (b) Who conquered Judah?

97. 2 Kings 24:18—25:30 *Memorize* Kings of Israel and Judah

    (a) Why did God deliver Judah to the Chaldeans?
    (b) What did Nebuzaradan do to the temple of the LORD?

98. Jeremiah 1

    (a) When did God appoint Jeremiah a prophet?
    (b) Jeremiah was afraid because he was a youth. Why shouldn't he be afraid?

99. Jeremiah 2 Test: 2 Kings 21–25

(a) What two sins had Judah committed?

(b) Why was Judah oppressed by other nations?

100. Jeremiah 4:1–26

(a) How could God's wrath be stopped?

(b) How did Jeremiah feel about God's punishment?

101. Jeremiah 5

(a) God asked Jeremiah to find a person in Jerusalem who dealt justly and sought the truth. How many did he find?

102. Jeremiah 7

(a) What building in Jerusalem comforted the people?

(b) What would happen to the temple?

103. Jeremiah 8

104. Jeremiah 9 *Memorize* Jeremiah 9:23–24

(a) What is worth boasting in?

105. Jeremiah 10

(a) Contrast the LORD and idols.

106. Jeremiah 11:18—12:17

(a) By chapter 11 and 12, which men started plotting evil against Jeremiah?

(b) Complete the sentence, "If you have raced with men on foot, and they have wearied you ..."

107. Jeremiah 13 <u>Test</u>: Jeremiah 1–10

(a) What did Jeremiah's ruined loincloth symbolize?

108. Jeremiah 14:1—15:4

(a) How did Jeremiah intercede for the people?

(b) God would not listen even if who interceded for the people?

109. Jeremiah 16

(a) It will no longer be said, "As the LORD lives who brought us up from the land of Egypt," but it will be said ...

110. Jeremiah 17

(a) Kings and princes would enter through the city gates, and the city would be inhabited forever if the people did what?

111. Jeremiah 18

   (a) If God declares a nation will be destroyed, and if that nation turns from evil, what will happen?

   (b) If God declares a nation will flourish, and if that nation does evil, what will happen?

112. Jeremiah 19–20   *Memorize* Jeremiah 17:5–10

   (a) What did Pashhur do to Jeremiah?

   (b) If Jeremiah said, "I will speak no more in the Lord's name," what happened?

113. Jeremiah 22

   (a) How did God answer this question: "Do you think you are a king because you compete in cedar?

114. Jeremiah 23

   (a) How were the prophets leading the people astray?

   (b) How can you tell that a prophet's words come from God?

115. Jeremiah 24:1—25:14   Test: Jeremiah 11–22

   (a) What did the good and bad figs mean?

   (b) How many years would Judah serve Babylon?

116. Jeremiah 26

   (a) Jeremiah prophesied in the Lord's house. What did the priests, prophets, and people plan?

   (b) Why did the officials and people defend Jeremiah?

117. Jeremiah 27

   (a) What did God make Jeremiah put around his neck?

   (b) What did the yoke mean?

118. Jeremiah 28

   (a) What did Hananiah prophesy, and what happened to him?

119. Jeremiah 29

   (a) What plans did God have for the exiles?

(b) What did God want the exiles to do?

120. Jeremiah 30

    (a) After God punished Judah, what did he plan?

121. Jeremiah 31

    (a) What will God's new covenant be like?

    (b) Under what circumstances would Israel cease to be a nation?

122. Jeremiah 32

    (a) Why did God want Jeremiah to buy a field?

123. Jeremiah 33   <u>Test</u>: Jeremiah 23–31

    (a) How certain was it that David's offspring would continue reigning over Israel?

124. Jeremiah 34

    (a) What covenant did Zedekiah and the people make about slaves, and why was God upset?

125. Jeremiah 35   *Memorize* Jeremiah 29:10–14

    (a) How were the Rechabites different than the people of Judah?

126. Jeremiah 36

    (a) Who wrote down Jeremiah's words?

    (b) How did people respond to Jeremiah's scroll?

    (c) What was Jehoiakim's punishment for burning the scroll?

127. Jeremiah 37

    (a) Why was Jeremiah thrown into prison (in the house of Jonathan the secretary)?

    (b) How was he released?

128. Jeremiah 38

    (a) Why did men throw Jeremiah into a cistern?

    (b) How was Jeremiah rescued from the cistern?

129. Jeremiah 39   <u>Test</u>: Jeremiah 32–38

    (a) What happened to Zedekiah after he was captured?

130. Jeremiah 40–41

(a) What happened to Gedaliah, governor of Judah?

(b) Who rescued the captives from Ishmael?

131. Jeremiah 42–43

   (a) What did God advise about going to Egypt?

   (b) What did Johanan do?

132. Jeremiah 44–45

   (a) What major sin did the Jews in Egypt commit?

133. Jeremiah 46–47

134. Jeremiah 48

135. Jeremiah 49

136. Jeremiah 50

137. Jeremiah 51

138. Jeremiah 52

   (a) What is the last thing Zedekiah saw?

   (b) What did Evil-merodach do for Jehoiachin?

139. Daniel 1   *Memorize* Daniel 2:20–23

   (a) Why were Daniel, Hananiah, Mishael, and Azariah in Babylon?

   (b) How were Daniel, Hananiah, Mishael, and Azariah better than the magicians and enchanters?

140. Daniel 2   <u>Test</u>: Jeremiah 39–52

   (a) Why did the king want the wise men killed?

   (b) To whom did God make known the dream?

   (c) Describe the statue and what it meant.

141. Daniel 3

   (a) Why was Nebuchadnezzar angry with Shadrach, Meshach, and Abednego?

   (b) What happened when Shadrach, Meshach, and Abednego were thrown in the furnace?

142. Daniel 4

   (a) After Nebuchadnezzar had the dream of a tree, what did Daniel advise?

(b) Why was Nebuchadnezzar driven from men and made to live with beasts?

143. Daniel 5

(a) What did Belshazzar do with the vessels of gold and silver from the temple?

(b) What was written on the wall, and what did it mean?

144. Daniel 6

(a) Why did the presidents and satraps seek a complaint against Daniel?

(b) Why didn't the lions eat Daniel?

145. Daniel 7 Test: Daniel 1–5

(a) What was different about the little horn?

(b) What was given to the son of man?

146. Daniel 8

(a) What nation did the ram represent?

(b) What nation did the goat represent?

147. Daniel 9

(a) After Daniel read Jeremiah, what did he do?

148. Daniel 10:1—11:13

(a) Why couldn't the man get to Daniel sooner?

149. Daniel 11:14—12:13

(a) At the end, what will happen to the dead?

150. Ezra 1:1—2:39 *Memorize* Ezra 3:10–13

(a) Why did Cyrus issue a decree to rebuild the temple?

151. Ezra 2:40—3:13 Test: Daniel 6–12

(a) What two sounds were heard as they laid the temple's foundation?

152. Ezra 4

(a) What did Artaxerxes decree about rebuilding Jerusalem?

153. Ezra 5–6

(a) What did Darius decree about rebuilding the temple?

(b) When was the temple completed?

154. Ezra 7

    (a) Why was God's hand with Ezra?

155. Ezra 8

156. Ezra 9:1—10:17

    (a) What sin greatly bothered Ezra?

    (b) What did the people do about this sin?

157. Nehemiah 1–2

    (a) When Nehemiah heard of Jerusalem's shame, what did he do?

    (b) How did the king help Nehemiah?

158. Nehemiah 3   <u>Test</u>: Ezra

159. Nehemiah 4

    (a) What measures did Nehemiah take to make sure reparations continued despite opposition?

160. Nehemiah 5

    (a) What were nobles doing when poor people couldn't pay tax?

161. Nehemiah 6:1—7:5

    (a) What did Shemaiah want Nehemiah to do?

162. Nehemiah 8   *Memorize* Nehemiah 8:5–6

    (a) How did the people respond after they heard the Law?

    (b) After they read the Law, what feast did they start?

163. Nehemiah 9:1–37

    (a) The Israelites confessed their sins. List some words that described God, and some words that described them.

164. Nehemiah 10–11

    (a) Name some parts of the covenant the people made with the Lord.

165. Nehemiah 12

166. Nehemiah 13   <u>Test</u>: Nehemiah

    (a) What sins did Nehemiah try to correct?

11 Year Two Maps and Tests

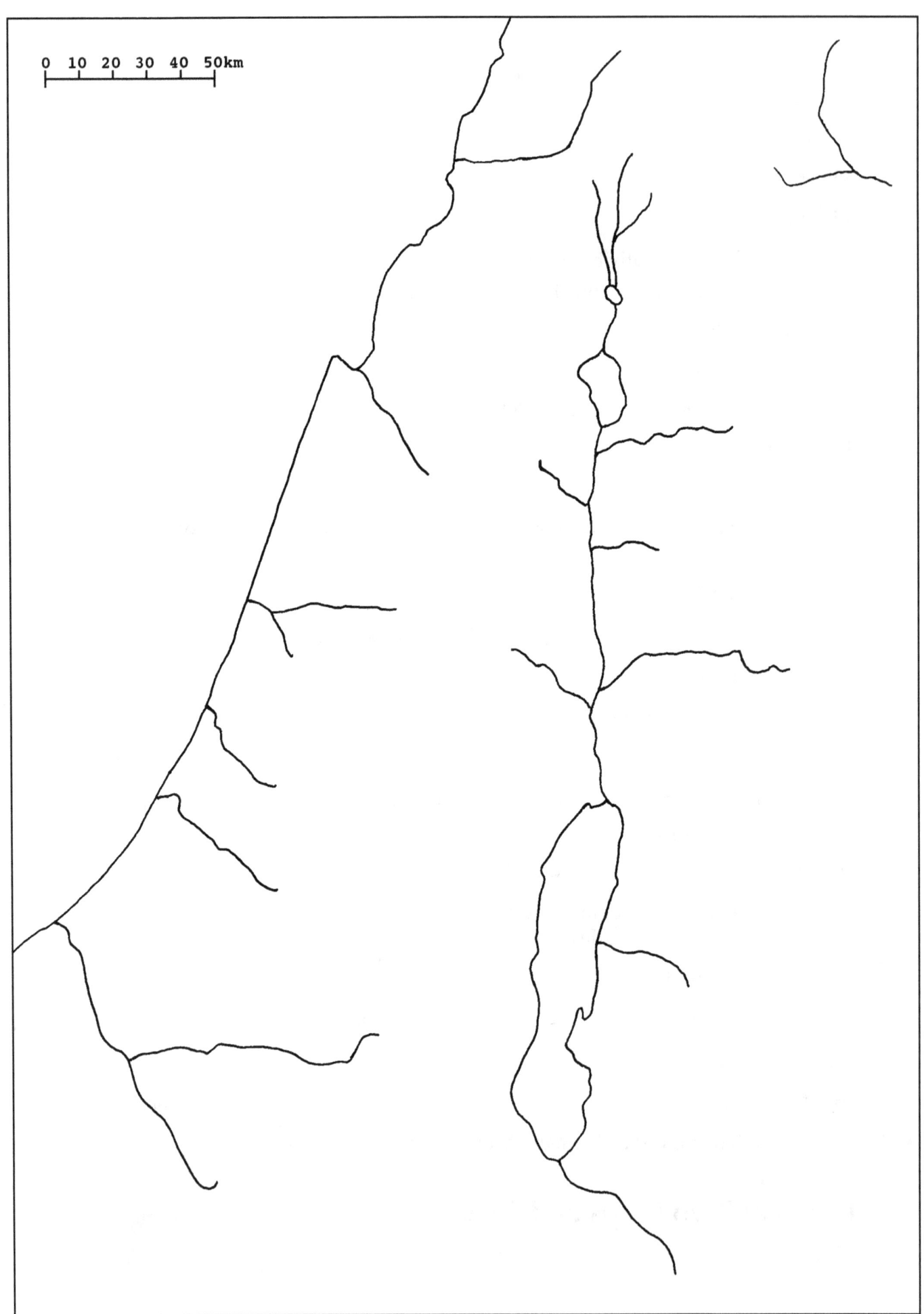

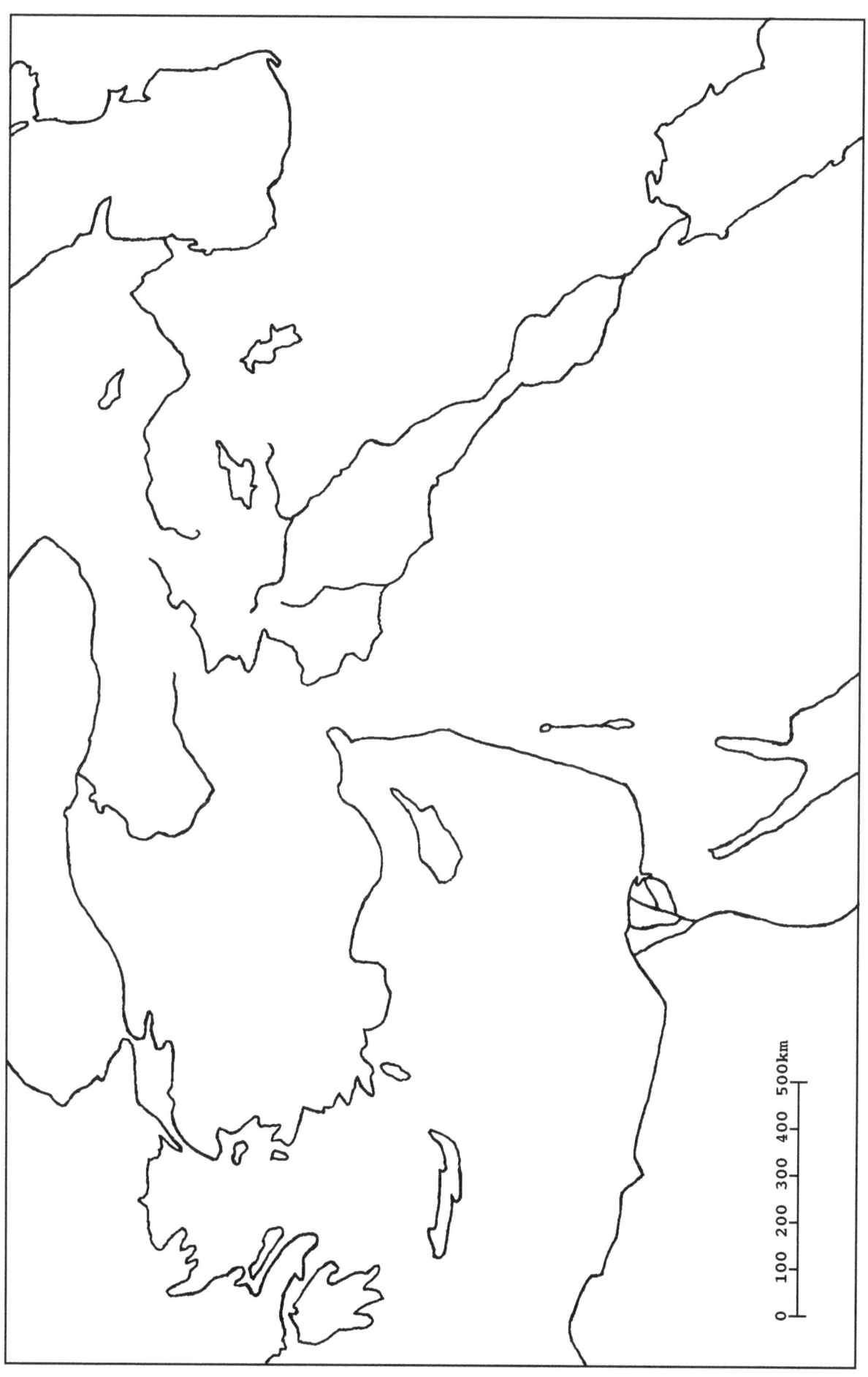

1 Samuel 1–8

Across
3 If you are returning to the LORD, put away your ____ gods.
5 The cows went straight toward ____.
8 The Philistines had the ark. God afflicted them with ____.
10 Eli and his sons died the same ____.
11 The people requested a ____.

Down
1 When God called Samuel, Samuel thought ____ called him.
2 Eli's sons treated the LORD's offering with ____.
4 Hannah vowed to ____ her son to the LORD.
5 Hannah was sad, because she was ____.
6 Those who honor me I will ____.
7 Elkanah had two wives: ____ and Peninnah.
9 Israel repented at ____.

1 Samuel 9–15

Directions: Circle the letter of the best answer.

1. Why did Saul come to Samuel's home town?

    (a) He was searching for donkeys.

    (b) He needed a place to stay.

    (c) God told him to go there.

    (d) He travelled there yearly.

2. Saul stayed with Samuel. What did Samuel not do for Saul?

    (a) told him about his donkeys

    (b) gave him something to eat

    (c) equipped him with a sword

    (d) anointed him king

3. God gave Saul a new what?

    (a) donkey

    (b) sword

    (c) crown

    (d) heart

4. At Mizpah, Saul was chosen by lot to be king. Where was Saul?

    (a) staying in Gibeah

    (b) hiding in the baggage

    (c) standing in the crowd

    (d) worshipping in Jerusalem

5. When Saul heard of Jabesh-gilead's trouble, what did he do?

    (a) gathered an army and freed the city

    (b) nothing

    (c) appointed Abner to free the city

    (d) prayed for God to send a deliverer

6. Samuel assembled the people at Gilgal. What sin did he confront them with?

    (a) worshipping idols

    (b) requesting a king

    (c) robbing the poor

    (d) hating their neighbor

7. Samuel asked God for a sign to reveal the sinfulness of Israel's action. What sign was it?

    (a) the sun stood still

    (b) the virgin conceived

    (c) thunder and rain came

    (d) enemies defeated them

8. Why would Saul's kingdom not continue?

    (a) He didn't wait for Samuel to offer a sacrifice.

    (b) He hated God.

    (c) He was jealous of David.

    (d) He didn't save the people of Michmash.

9. The Philistines camped at Michmash. What showed the Israelites were hard pressed?

   (a) They were outnumbered, and God wasn't with them.
   (b) God wasn't with them, and they lacked weapons.
   (c) They were old, and they were afraid.
   (d) They were outnumbered, and they lacked weapons.

10. How did God work through Jonathan and his armor-bearer?

    (a) He brought about a victory over the Philistines.
    (b) He brought about repentance in the land.
    (c) He brought new weapons for the army.
    (d) He brought many soldiers from Gilead.

11. What harmful vow did Saul make?

    (a) no one shall fight but Benjamin
    (b) no one shall drink
    (c) no one shall eat
    (d) no one shall worship

12. How did Saul disobey God's command about the Amalekites?

    (a) He made peace with them.
    (b) He left some things alive.
    (c) He destroyed their army.
    (d) He worshipped their gods.

13. "Because you have rejected the word of the LORD,

    (a) he has punished you with plague."
    (b) he has withdrawn his blessing."
    (c) he has forgiven you."
    (d) he has rejected you from being king."

1 Samuel 16–20

Directions: Fill in the blanks.

1. "Man looks on the outward appearance, but the LORD looks on the _____."

2. Samuel anointed _____ king after Saul.

3. David played the _____ when an evil spirit tormented Saul.

4. David brought food to his _____ in the army.

5. _____ challenged the armies of Israel.

6. David had defeated a lion and a _____ with God's help.

7. "You come to me with sword and spear, but I come to you in the name of the _____."

8. David defeated Goliath with a _____ and stone.

9. David married _____, Saul's daughter.

10. "Saul has struck down his _____, and David his ten _____."

11. Saul was _____ of David's popularity.

12. Saul planned to kill David the first time. _____ spoke with Saul and changed his mind.

13. Instead of capturing David at Naioth, Saul _____.

14. Saul's _____ proved to Jonathan that his father meant to harm David.

15. Jonathan shot _____ to inform David of his findings.

1 Samuel 21—2 Samuel 1

Directions: Answer in complete sentences.

1. How did Ahimelech of Nob help David?

2. How was Keilah saved from the Philistines?

3. Why did David not harm Saul?

4. David planned to kill Nabal's household. Why did he change his mind?

5. Saul slept on the hill of Hachilah. What did David do?

6. After David spared Saul, why did he flee to Gath?

7. The Philistines gathered at Aphek. Why did Saul consult a medium?

8. When David returned from Aphek, what was wrong with Ziklag?

_____

_____

9. How did Saul die?

_____

_____

2 Samuel 2–10

```
M F D I S H B O S H E T H
E N L L C D S T L A M U E
P S O P L A S Y E I L E O
H E B R O N T H P N K C J
I R Z G J C A Q T I T H O
B Z N F E E H H C M K P A
O D R L L D R Y Z C A R B
S O K B Y O Y U G I M O T
H T G F W Q D Z S X H M B
E L L O U U X Z R A M I U
T N U J D A S A H E L S I
H B H L L O S H D V H E O
D V H X U J U M B K X D M
```

1. David moved from Ziklag to __ __ __ __ __ __.

2. Abner set up __ __ __ __ __ __ __ __ __ __ as king.

3. Abner killed __ __ __ __ __ __ (Joab's brother) in battle.

4. __ __ __ __ murdered Abner.

5. Ish-bosheth was murdered as he __ __ __ __ __ __.

6. David conquered the Jebusites and moved to __ __ __ __ __ __ __ __ __.

7. __ __ __ __ __ died after touching the ark.

8. Michal was angry, because David __ __ __ __ __ __ before the LORD mightily.

9. David was troubled, because he dwelt in a palace, and the ark dwelt in a __ __ __ __.

10. God _ _ _ _ _ _ _ _ David that his kingdom would never end.

11. David was victorious, because _ _ _ was with him.

12. David treated Jonathan's son, _ _ _ _ _ _ _ _ _ _ _, kindly.

2 Samuel 11–18

Summarize the story of David, Bathsheba and Absalom. Tell only the major events.

2 Samuel 19–24

Across
2 God punished Israel, because David took a ____.
3 God caused a ____, because Saul hurt the Gibeonites.
6 The tribe of ____ first brought David back as king.
7 David chose ____ to lead the army instead of Joab.

Down
1 ____ saved David from Ishbi-benob.
4 David had 37 ____ men.
5 David's three mightiest men were Josheb-basshebeth, ____ and Shammah.
8 David wrote a ____, when the LORD delivered him.

1 Kings 1–8

Directions: Circle the letter of the best answer.

1. Who plotted to become king after David?
   - (a) Joab
   - (b) Benaiah
   - (c) Adonijah
   - (d) Chileab

2. Who told David about the plot?
   - (a) Solomon
   - (b) Nathan
   - (c) Bathsheba
   - (d) (b) and (c)

3. Before David died, he commanded Solomon to
   - (a) keep the law of the LORD.
   - (b) marry few wives.
   - (c) show Shimei kindness.
   - (d) bury him in Bethlehem.

4. What four men did Solomon punish?
   - (a) Benaiah, Barzillai, Zadok, Nathan
   - (b) Abiathar, Joab, Adonijah, Shimei
   - (c) Benaiah, Barzillai, Abiathar, Joab
   - (d) Zadok, Nathan, Adonijah, Shimei

5. God appeared to Solomon in a dream. What did Solomon request?
   - (a) wealth
   - (b) honor
   - (c) power
   - (d) wisdom

6. Two mothers fought over a child. Solomon commanded the child be
   - (a) adopted.
   - (b) sawn in two.
   - (c) given to the first mother.
   - (d) given to the second mother.

7. Why did people from all nations come to Solomon?
   - (a) to hear his wisdom
   - (b) to pay him tribute
   - (c) to trade with him
   - (d) to make treaties with him

8. With whom did Solomon make a treaty?
   - (a) Hadad the Edomite
   - (b) Jeroboam son of Nebat
   - (c) Hiram king of Tyre
   - (d) Ben-hadad king of Assyria

9. How many years did it take Solomon to complete the temple?
   - (a) 3
   - (b) 5
   - (c) 7
   - (d) 9

10. Besides the temple, Solomon built

    (a) palaces
    (b) cities
    (c) walls
    (d) all of the above

11. What skillful worker from Tyre helped build the temple furnishings?

    (a) Hiram
    (b) Bezalel
    (c) Noah
    (d) Kenaniah

12. What filled the temple after the ark was placed in it?

    (a) many people
    (b) some blood
    (c) a cloud
    (d) a fire

13. Solomon stood before the altar in front of the people and

    (a) remained silent.
    (b) advised them.
    (c) listened.
    (d) prayed.

14. In Solomon's prayer, what was the people's biggest problem?

    (a) sin
    (b) famine
    (c) enemies
    (d) locust

15. How did the people feel after the temple's dedication?

    (a) guilty
    (b) joyful
    (c) indifferent
    (d) angry

1 Kings 9–16

Directions: Fill in the blanks.

1. The LORD promised to establish Solomon's throne _____, if Solomon obeyed the LORD's commands.

2. The Queen of _____ came to hear Solomon's wisdom.

3. Solomon _____ many foreign women.

4. God raised _____ to punish Solomon.

5. Rehoboam said, "My father laid on you a heavy _____. I will add to your _____."

6. Jeroboam worried people would sacrifice in Jerusalem, so he built golden _____

7. A man of God prophesied _____ would sacrifice the false priests on Jeroboam's altar.

8. A _____ killed the man of God, because he disobeyed the LORD.

9. _____ prophesied that Israel would be rooted up and scattered, because of their sin.

10. Shishak, king of Egypt, came against Jerusalem and _____ the treasures of the house of the LORD.

11. Asa _____ the false gods' altars and commanded Judah to _____ the LORD.

12. When Baasha threatened Judah, Asa asked _____ for help.

13. _____ destroyed Jeroboam's family.

14. Ahab did more _____ than all the kings before him.

1 Kings 17–22

Directions: Answer in complete sentences.

1. When they first met, what did Elijah tell Ahab?

2. In what two ways did God provide for Elijah during the drought?

3. In the contest on Mount Carmel, how would the true God prove himself?

4. At Horeb, how did God appear to Elijah?

5. What three tasks did God give Elijah at Horeb?

2 Chronicles 17–21, 2 Kings 1–2

```
Y  R  U  F  E  H  B  S  P  I  R  I  T  J
O  O  N  L  N  E  D  R  M  F  S  B  M  T
T  M  I  Y  M  A  N  E  Z  Z  L  N  I  K
H  V  Z  I  P  V  D  H  Z  G  E  L  F  Y
E  Y  V  K  J  E  X  C  C  P  W  R  F  B
R  G  P  F  Y  N  Y  A  V  B  O  S  I  A
B  T  B  A  A  L  Z  E  B  U  B  P  D  F
I  I  R  Z  I  D  X  T  Z  M  A  H  V  C
R  P  I  X  N  P  R  F  F  E  H  B  U  P
M  D  D  N  G  O  X  I  H  N  A  G  S  E
```

1. Jehoshaphat sought the LORD, appointed _ _ _ _ _ _ _ _, and appointed judges.

2. God did not like Jehoshaphat's alliance with _ _ _ _.

3. A great army came against Judah. Jehoshaphat sought the LORD, proclaimed a fast and _ _ _ _ _ _.

4. The army against Judah destroyed each _ _ _ _ _.

5. Ahaziah consulted _ _ _ _ _ _ _ _ _, god of Ekron, rather than the LORD.

6. _ _ _ _ came down from heaven and consumed the captain and his 50 men.

7. Jehoshaphat's son, Jehoram, did what was _ _ _ _ _.

8. God punished Jehoram with rebellions, invaders, and a disease of the _ _ _ _ _ _.

9. Elijah was taken to _ _ _ _ _ _ in a whirlwind.

10. Elisha requested a double portion of Elijah's _ _ _ _ _ _.

2 Kings 3–7

List the miracles God performed through Elisha for the woman from Shunem.

_____
_____
_____
_____
_____
_____
_____
_____

Tell the story of the king of Syria's attempt to capture Elisha.

_____
_____
_____
_____
_____
_____
_____
_____

2 Kings 8–13, 2 Chronicles 22–24

Across
2 _____ murdered Joram and became king.
3 Athaliah seized the throne of _____.
4 Jehu followed the sins of _____.
7 Jehoiada helped Joash become _____.
8 Joash repaired the _____.
9 Jehu ended _____ worship.

Down
1 Hazael _____ Ben-hadad and became king of Syria.
4 Joash murdered Zechariah, son of _____.
5 A dead man arose, when he fell on the _____ of Elisha.
6 Elisha had a man _____ Jehu king.

2 Kings 14–20

Directions: Circle the letter of the best answer.

1. What did Amaziah do with Edom's gods?

    (a) worshipped them

    (b) burned them

    (c) challenged them

    (d) nothing

2. What did Uzziah do in the days of Zechariah?

    (a) built a wall

    (b) defeated the Philistines

    (c) sought the LORD

    (d) buried his son

3. Why did God strike Uzziah with leprosy?

    (a) Uzziah murdered a prophet.

    (b) Uzziah forsook the LORD.

    (c) Uzziah worshipped Baal.

    (d) Uzziah burned incense in the temple.

4. Which nation began to trouble Israel during the reign of Menahem?

    (a) Syria

    (b) Babylon

    (c) Assyria

    (d) Ammon

5. When Rezin and Pekah came against Judah, whom did Ahaz ask for help?

    (a) the LORD

    (b) Assyria

    (c) Egypt

    (d) Edom

6. It is not recorded that Ahaz

    (a) burned his son as an offering.

    (b) worshipped the god of Syria.

    (c) sacrificed on the high places.

    (d) married a foreign woman.

7. Why was Israel conquered and exiled?

    (a) Israel sinned.

    (b) Israel had a weak army.

    (c) Israel's alliances were weak.

    (d) Israel cruelly treated conquered nations.

8. Which god did the Samaritans serve?

    (a) the LORD

    (b) their own gods

    (c) both (a) and (b)

    (d) none of the above

9. What kind of king was Hezekiah?

    (a) good

    (b) evil

    (c) mediocre

    (d) crazy

10. What did the Rabshekah of Assyria declare about the LORD?

    (a) He is the true God.

    (b) He is a false god.

    (c) He doesn't care.

    (d) He cannot deliver Judah.

11. Which prophet reassured Hezekiah?

    (a) Micah

    (b) Isaiah

    (c) Jeremiah

    (d) Ezekiel

12. Why were the Assyrians forced to leave?

    (a) An angel slew much of their army.

    (b) Hezekiah's army was stronger.

    (c) They exhausted their food and water.

    (d) The Babylonians attacked Nineveh.

13. What sign did God work to show Hezekiah he would live longer?

    (a) A virgin conceived.

    (b) Food prices dropped.

    (c) A shadow went forward.

    (d) A shadow went backward.

14. What did Isaiah say Babylon would do?

    (a) take away the king's things

    (b) be defeated by Assyria

    (c) seek the LORD

    (d) defeat Samaria

2 Kings 21–25

Directions: Fill in the blanks.

1. Manasseh was more _____ than the Amorites.

2. Prophets predicted _____ upon Judah, because of Manasseh's actions.

3. Hilkiah found the _____.

4. _____ tore his clothes when he heard God's words.

5. Josiah destroyed the _____ at Bethel.

6. Josiah _____ in battle with Pharaoh Neco.

7. Kings records Judah was first captured during the reign of _____.

8. _____ conquered Judah.

9. God delivered Judah to oppressors because _____.

10. Nebuzaradan _____ the house of the LORD.

Jeremiah 1–10

Directions: Answer in complete sentences.

1. When did God appoint Jeremiah a prophet?

2. Judah committed two sins, and God likened them to water. What were the two sins, and how did each relate to water?

3. What building in Jerusalem comforted the people, and what would happen to it?

4. What is not worth boasting in, and what is worth boasting in?

5. Contrast the Lord and idols.

Jeremiah 11–22

```
C  V  E  E  F  N  L  G  C  Q  P  J
P  S  T  S  R  I  T  L  P  F  A  O
X  F  S  B  V  P  R  I  D  E  S  M
U  F  A  E  Q  G  O  E  Z  C  H  J
A  F  M  G  S  A  B  B  A  T  H  M
Q  R  U  O  I  R  T  X  M  Y  U  Q
C  Z  E  I  R  Y  O  A  V  C  R  W
R  E  L  E  N  T  L  H  T  R  O  N
```

1. By chapter 11, men planned _ _ _ _ against Jeremiah.

2. If you have raced with men on foot, and they have wearied you, how will you compete with _ _ _ _ _ _ ?

3. Jeremiah's ruined loincloth symbolized the ruined _ _ _ _ _ of Judah.

4. Even if Moses and _ _ _ _ _ _ stood before the LORD, God would not turn to the people.

5. It will no longer be said, "As the LORD lives who brought us up from the land of Egypt," but it will be said, "As the LORD lives who brought us up from the _ _ _ _ _ ."

6. Kings and princes would enter through the city gates, and the city would be inhabited forever if the people kept the _ _ _ _ _ _ _ .

7. If God declares a nation will be destroyed, and if that nation turns from evil, God will _ _ _ _ _ _ .

224

8. _ _ _ _ _ _ _ beat Jeremiah and put him in stocks.

9. If Jeremiah said, "I will speak no more in God's name," God's word felt like a _ _ _ _ inside of him.

Jeremiah 23–31

How can you tell a prophet's words are from God?

How were the people of Judah like good and bad figs?

Tell the story of Jeremiah's yoke. Make sure to include Hananiah.

Jeremiah 32–38

Across
2 King _____ burned Jeremiah's scroll.
4 _____ rescued Jeremiah from the cistern.
7 God's covenant with _____ was as sure as his covenant with the day and night.
8 Zedekiah and the people promised to free _____, but they broke the promise.
9 To show the land would be restored, God asked Jeremiah to buy a _____.
10 The Rechabites refused _____.

Down
1 _____ wrote Jeremiah's words.
3 King _____ released Jeremiah from prison.
5 The officials threw Jeremiah into prison. They thought he was _____ to the Babylonians.
6 Jeremiah promised a better state for those who went to the Chaldeans. The officials threw him into a _____.

Jeremiah 39–52

Directions: Circle the letter of the best answer.

1. What happened to Zedekiah after he was captured?

    (a) His eyes were put out.

    (b) He was killed.

    (c) He escaped.

    (d) He repented.

2. What did Ishmael do?

    (a) He sought the LORD.

    (b) He destroyed the temple.

    (c) He helped Jeremiah.

    (d) He murdered Gedaliah.

3. What did Johanan do?

    (a) He rescued captives from Ishmael.

    (b) He warned Gedaliah.

    (c) He fled to Egypt.

    (d) all of the above

4. What did God advise about going to Egypt?

    (a) In Egypt, you will be blessed with the fruit of field and womb.

    (b) In Egypt, you will lead Egyptians from their false gods.

    (c) In Egypt, you will die by sword, famine and pestilence.

    (d) In Egypt, you will seek and find the LORD.

5. What major sin did the Jews in Egypt commit?

    (a) adultery

    (b) idolatry

    (c) Sabbath breaking

    (d) murder

6. Over which nations did Jeremiah prophesy judgment?

    (a) Egypt, Persia, Moab, Syria, Edom, Spain

    (b) Cyprus, Philistia, Syria, Ammon, Sheba, Babylon

    (c) Egypt, Philistia, Moab, Ammon, Edom, Babylon

    (d) Rome, Persia, Mesopotamia, Amalek, Cyprus, Babel

7. What's the last thing Zedekiah saw?

    (a) his sons slaughtered

    (b) the temple destroyed

    (c) an angel

    (d) the wall broken through

8. What did Evil-merodach do for Jehoiachin?

    (a) released him from prison

    (b) gave him a house

    (c) made him governor

    (d) all of the above

Daniel 1–5

Directions: Fill in the blanks.

1. Daniel, Hananiah, _____, and Azariah were exiles from Judah, living in Babylon.

2. Nebuchadnezzar found Daniel and his friends ten times better in _____ and understanding than the magicians and enchanters.

3. The magicians and enchanters could not tell king Nebuchadnezzar a dream; therefore, Nebuchadnezzar wanted them _____.

4. God told the dream to _____.

5. The statue was made of _____, silver, _____, and iron.

6. Each part of the statue represented a _____.

7. Shadrach, Meschach and Abednego refused to _____ the image of gold.

8. Nebuchadnezzar saw _____ men in the furnace.

9. Nebuchadnezzar had a dream about a _____. Daniel advised Nebuchadnezzar to stop sinning and practice righteousness.

10. Nebuchadnezzar was driven from men and lived with _____.

11. The _____ rules the kingdoms of men and sets over them whomever he pleases.

Daniel 6–12

Directions: Answer in complete sentences.

1. Why was Daniel thrown into a lions' den?

   _____

   _____

2. Why didn't the lions eat Daniel?

   _____

   _____

3. What was given to the son of man?

   _____

   _____

4. What nations did the ram and goat represent?

   _____

   _____

5. After Daniel read Jeremiah, what did he do?

   _____

   _____

Ezra

```
I Y P Z W W S T V N G K E
A N D M B P E D J G L Z E
F B T J N N E T O K H T A
D J I E J C Y S P D Y S A
Z L X U R J Q B R E K V R
T P F O S M T H X H W T E
L I V Y D V A T R S W Z T
F I H W O Q U R L I D E X
D A R I U S G X R N P V Q
Q L Y E U D H X X I X S W
Y D Y R N I T R V F A G E
W K Y R X I I O G U J G X
U C F A D G S B A B O Z E
```

1. _ _ _ _ _ issued a decree to rebuild the temple.

2. After they laid the foundation, people shouted and _ _ _ _ _.

3. The Jews ceased building the temple and restarted during the reign of _ _ _ _ _ _.

4. The temple was _ _ _ _ _ _ _ _ on the third day of Adar in the sixth year of Darius's reign.

5. God's hand was with Ezra, because he studied, practiced and _ _ _ _ _ _ the Law of God.

6. What sin greatly bothered Ezra? _ _ _ _ _ _ _ _ _ _ _ _

7. Men _ _ _ _ _ _ _ their wives to correct the sin.

231

Nehemiah

How did Nehemiah go from cupbearer to governor?

What opposition occurred as the Jews repaired the wall, and how did Nehemiah handle it?

After reading the Law, what changes occurred?

Part V

Year Three
(Esther through Malachi, sans Psalms, Jeremiah, Daniel, and Obadiah)

12 Year Three Plan

1. Esther 1   *Memorize* Esther 4:12–17

   (a) How did Vashti upset Ahaseurus?

   (b) How did Ahaseurus handle Vashti's actions?

2. Esther 2

   (a) What was Esther's nationality?

   (b) Why was Esther made queen?

3. Esther 3–4

   (a) What did Haman plot?

   (b) What did Esther plan to do about it?

4. Esther 5:1—6:13

   (a) Did Ahaseurus extend the golden scepter to Esther?

   (b) How did Ahaseurus honor Mordecai?

5. Esther 6:14—8:17

   (a) Whose side did king Ahaseurus take after Esther exposed Haman's plot?

   (b) Haman's edict was not revoked. Why did the Jews celebrate?

6. Esther 9–10

   (a) Who gained mastery on the thirteenth day of the twelfth month?

   (b) What holiday do Jews celebrate, remembering the events in Esther?

7. Job 1

   (a) What kind of man was Job?

   (b) Why did Satan think Job feared God?

8. Job 2   <u>Test</u>: Esther

   (a) How did Satan harm Job the second time?

   (b) After Job was harmed, how did he act toward God?

   (c) Who came to comfort Job?

9. Job 3   *Memorize* Job 1:20–22

   (a) What did Job wish about his birth?

10. Job 4–5

11. Job 6

12. Job 7–8

13. Job 9

14. Job 10–11

15. Job 12 <u>Test</u>: Job 1–10

16. Job 13–14

17. Job 18–19 *Memorize* Job 38:1–7

18. Job 31

19. Job 32–33

    (a) Why did Job's three friends cease to answer Job?

    (b) Who spoke after Job's three friends?

20. Job 34

21. Job 38

    (a) After Elihu spoke, who spoke?

    (b) What are some questions the Lord asked Job?

22. Job 39–40

    (a) What animals does God describe?

    (b) God asked, "Shall the faultfinder contend with the Almighty? He who argues with God, let him answer it." How did Job respond?

23. Job 41

    (a) When God describes Leviathan, what is he telling Job?

24. Job 42

    (a) What did Job say after God questioned him?

    (b) How did Job help his three friends?

    (c) How did God treat Job after their encounter?

25. Proverbs 1 *Memorize* Proverbs 3:1–20

    (a) Who wrote Proverbs?

    (b) What are the Proverbs for?

    (c) What is the beginning of knowledge?

26. Proverbs 2   <u>Test</u>: Job 11–42

    (a) If you seek wisdom and understanding, what will happen?

27. Proverbs 3

    (a) Complete the Proverb: Trust in the LORD with all your heart . . .

28. Proverbs 4

29. Proverbs 5

    (a) Solomon says, "Keep your way from her, and do not go near the door of her house." About whom is he speaking?

30. Proverbs 6

31. Proverbs 7

32. Proverbs 8

33. Proverbs 9

34. Proverbs 10

35. Proverbs 11   <u>Test</u>: Proverbs 1–9

36. Proverbs 12

37. Proverbs 13

38. Proverbs 15

39. Proverbs 16

40. Proverbs 17

41. Proverbs 18–19

42. Proverbs 20

43. Proverbs 21

44. Proverbs 23

45. Proverbs 24

46. Proverbs 26–27   *Memorize* Ecclesiastes 3:9–15

47. Proverbs 28–29

48. Proverbs 30

49. Proverbs 31 <u>Test</u>: Proverbs 10–31

50. Ecclesiastes 1

    (a) When the preacher observed things in the world, he said, "all is ____."

    (b) The preacher gained wisdom, but he found "in much wisdom is much ____."

51. Ecclesiastes 2

    (a) What did the preacher discover after he sought pleasure?

    (b) When you toil, what happens to your work after your death?

52. Ecclesiastes 3

    (a) Name some things for which there is a time.

    (b) Solomon said, "there is nothing better for [man] than to ..."

53. Ecclesiastes 4–5

    (a) Why are two better than one?

    (b) Why should you not be hasty to speak to God?

54. Ecclesiastes 6:1—7:13

    (a) A man has many children and lives many years, but he is not satisfied with life and has no burial. Who is better off than he?

55. Ecclesiastes 7:14—8:17

    (a) Solomon saw a vanity: "righteous people perishing but wicked people ____."

56. Ecclesiastes 9

    (a) With what person should a man enjoy life?

    (b) After the poor wise man delivered the city, how was he treated?

57. Ecclesiastes 10 *Memorize* Ecclesiastes 12:13–14

58. Ecclesiastes 11–12

    (a) How well do we know the work of God?

    (b) What should we remember in our youth?

    (c) What is the end of the matter?

59. Song of Solomon 1–2 <u>Test</u>: Ecclesiastes

    (a) Who are the two main characters in Song of Solomon?

    (b) What skin-color was Solomon's lover?

60. Song of Solomon 3–4

   (a) What does the bride adjure the daughters of Jerusalem?

61. Song of Solomon 5–6

   (a) How does the bride describe her beloved's appearance?

   (b) How does Solomon describe his bride's appearance?

62. Song of Solomon 7–8

   (a) Love is as strong as ____.

63. Isaiah 1   *Memorize* Isaiah 1:12–20

   (a) "From the sole of the foot to the head, there is no soundness in it, but bruises and sores and raw wounds." What is Isaiah speaking about?

   (b) Why did God despise Israel's offerings, sacrifices, assemblies, and prayers?

   (c) How will Zion be redeemed?

64. Isaiah 2   <u>Test</u>: Song of Solomon

   (a) In the latter days, what will the mountain of the house of the LORD be like?

   (b) What shall happen to the pride of man?

65. Isaiah 3–4

   (a) What will happen to the women's finery?

   (b) What will the land be like after God judges it?

66. Isaiah 5

   (a) How were Jerusalem and Judah compared to a vineyard?

   (b) God says, "Woe to those who …" Name some of the "who's."

67. Isaiah 6–7

   (a) How did Isaiah feel after he saw God on his throne and the seraphim?

   (b) Why was Ahaz afraid?

   (c) Ahaz didn't ask for a sign, but God would give him a sign. What was the sign?

68. Isaiah 8

   (a) Whom should Isaiah fear?

69. Isaiah 9   <u>Test</u>: Isaiah 1–7

   (a) Who would see a great light?

(b) Why would the warrior's clothing be burned?

70. Isaiah 10

    (a) How was Assyria like an axe?

71. Isaiah 11–12

    (a) What kind of Spirit shall rest on the shoot of Jesse?

72. Isaiah 13

    (a) When God punishes Babylon, how many people will there be?

73. Isaiah 14

74. Isaiah 17–18

75. Isaiah 22

    (a) What position would Eliakim, son of Hilkiah, take?

76. Isaiah 23

77. Isaiah 24   <u>Test</u>: Isaiah 8–23

    (a) What will the LORD do to the earth?

    (b) What will people in the west and east do?

78. Isaiah 25–26   *Memorize* Isaiah 9:2–7

    (a) What will God swallow up on the mountain of the LORD?

    (b) Complete the sentence, "If favor is shown to the wicked, he does not learn ____."

79. Isaiah 28

    (a) What did God's words sound like to those who would not hear?

    (b) God will lay a cornerstone in Zion. What will justice and righteousness be like?

80. Isaiah 29

    (a) People drew near to God with their mouths and honored God with their lips. What was wrong?

81. Isaiah 30

    (a) From what nation did people seek help?

82. Isaiah 32

(a) What kind of woman does Isaiah address in Isaiah 32?

83. Isaiah 33

(a) Who can dwell with the consuming fire?

84. Isaiah 36 <u>Test</u>: Isaiah 24–33

(a) Why wouldn't the Rabshakeh speak in Aramaic?

(b) In the king of Assyria's mind, what was the LORD unable to do?

85. Isaiah 37

(a) When Hezekiah received the Rabshakeh's letter, what did he do?

(b) How did God stop Sennacherib?

86. Isaiah 38–39

(a) When Hezekiah heard he would die, he prayed. How did God answer him?

(b) Who sent an envoy, congratulating Hezekiah on his recovery?

87. Isaiah 40

(a) Complete the sentence, "The grass withers, the flower fades, but ..."

(b) To whom can God be compared?

88. Isaiah 41

(a) "Fear not, for I am with you; be not dismayed, for I am your God." To whom is God speaking?

(b) When the poor and needy seek water, what will God do?

89. Isaiah 42

(a) "God's servant will not grow faint or be discouraged till ..."

(b) Who gave Jacob to the looter and plunderer?

90. Isaiah 44

(a) A carpenter chops down a cedar. He uses a part for fuel. What does he do with the other part?

91. Isaiah 45 <u>Test</u>: Isaiah 34–42

(a) Who declared things to come long ago?

(b) Whom should all the earth turn to, to be saved?

92. Isaiah 46–47

(a) What two things would come upon the daughter of the Chaldeans?

(b) What did the daughter of the Chaldeans say in her heart?

93. Isaiah 49   *Memorize* Isaiah 40:27–31

(a) Not only would the servant restore Israel, he would be a ____ for the nations.

(b) Zion said, "the LORD has forgotten me." How did God respond? (Use the image.)

94. Isaiah 50–51

(a) What should people do if they fear the LORD and obey his servant?

(b) What should those who know righteousness not fear?

95. Isaiah 52–53

(a) Why was God's servant wounded and crushed?

(b) After the servant dies, what will he do?

96. Isaiah 54–55

(a) What will God's word do that goes out from his mouth?

(b) The mountains may depart and the hills be removed, but what about God's steadfast love for Israel?

97. Isaiah 56–57

(a) List some things God says about the foreigner in Isaiah 56.

(b) Why do some righteous people perish?

98. Isaiah 58   Test: Isaiah 43–55

(a) Why didn't God acknowledge the people's fasting?

(b) What kind of fast did God want?

99. Isaiah 59

(a) Why did God not hear their prayers?

(b) God was displeased that there was no ____.

100. Isaiah 60   *Memorize* Isaiah 55:6–9

(a) "Arise, shine, for your light has come, and the ____."

(b) Why will the sun not be needed for light?

101. Isaiah 61–62

(a) The Spirit of the LORD was upon him, because the LORD anointed him to do what?

102. Isaiah 63–64

(a) Why were God's garments red?

(b) Why were the people unclean, fading like a leaf, and God hid his face from them?

103. Isaiah 65

(a) To whom did God spread out his hands all day?

(b) God will create new what?

104. Isaiah 66

(a) To whom will God look?

105. Lamentations 1

(a) The city full of people is like a widow. To which city does the author refer?

(b) What was Zion like after the punishment?

106. Lamentations 2 <u>Test</u>: Isaiah 56–66

107. Lamentations 3

(a) Why was there hope?

(b) "Why should a living man complain about ____."

108. Lamentations 4–5

(a) Jerusalem's chastisement was greater than what?

(b) Why were the victims of the sword happier than the victims of hunger?

109. Ezekiel 1–2 *Memorize* Lamentations 3:21–24

(a) Describe what Ezekiel saw.

(b) What word did God use to describe the house of Israel?

110. Ezekiel 3 <u>Test</u>: Lamentations

(a) How was Ezekiel like a watchman?

111. Ezekiel 4–5

(a) Why did Ezekiel build a Jerusalem model? What was he symbolizing?

(b) What did God command Ezekiel to do with his hair, and what did it symbolize?

112. Ezekiel 6–7

    (a) When God punishes Judah, where will the slain bodies be?

113. Ezekiel 8–9

    (a) How did Ezekiel get to Jerusalem?

    (b) What did Ezekiel see in Jerusalem?

114. Ezekiel 10 *Memorize* Ezekiel 7:23–27

    (a) What did the man clothed in linen scatter over the city?

115. Ezekiel 11

    (a) Those in Jerusalem thought the land was for them, and the exiles were far from the LORD. What did God plan?

    (b) What would God give the exiles when they returned?

116. Ezekiel 12

    (a) Why did Ezekiel prepare an exile's baggage and go into exile by day?

    (b) The people quoted a proverb: "The days grow long, and every vision comes to nothing." What did God say?

117. Ezekiel 13

    (a) Where did the false prophets claim their words came from?

118. Ezekiel 14–15 <u>Test</u>: Ezekiel 1–11

    (a) What will God do to those who worship idols yet still inquire of God?

    (b) When a land sins against the LORD, if Noah, Daniel and Job were in it, whom could they save?

119. Ezekiel 16

    (a) Israel is like a woman. How did God care for her?

    (b) Israel is like a woman. How did they respond to God's help?

120. Ezekiel 17

    (a) An eagle planted a twig. How did the twig grow?

    (b) How was Zedekiah like the twig?

121. Ezekiel 18

    (a) What was wrong with the proverb, "The fathers have eaten sour grapes, and the children's teeth are set on edge"?

(b) The LORD has no pleasure in the death of anyone. He wants people to ____.

122. Ezekiel 20　　　　　　　　　　　　　　　　　　*Memorize* Ezekiel 18:30–32

   (a) What was in Israel's mind that would never happen?

123. Ezekiel 22　　　　　　　　　　　　　　　　　　<u>Test</u>: Ezekiel 12–20

   (a) List some sins Israel committed.

   (b) How was Israel like dross of silver?

124. Ezekiel 23

   (a) Who were Oholah and Oholibah?

   (b) How did Oholah and Oholibah behave?

125. Ezekiel 24

   (a) What happened in the ninth year, tenth month, and tenth day of their exile?

   (b) Ezekiel's wife died, and the LORD commanded him not to mourn. Why?

126. Ezekiel 25–26

   (a) Why would God punish Ammon?

   (b) Why would God punish Edom and Philistia?

127. Ezekiel 29–30

   (a) What did Ezekiel prophesy about Egypt?

   (b) Nebuchadnezzar labored hard against Tyre, but he didn't capture it. What did God pay him?

128. Ezekiel 33

   (a) The inhabitants of the waste places said, "Abraham was only one man, yet he got possession of the land; but we are many; the land is surely given us to possess." What was wrong with their thinking?

129. Ezekiel 34　　　　　　　　　　　　　　　　　　*Memorize* Ezekiel 37:11–14

   (a) What were the shepherds doing to the flock?

   (b) What would God do about the evil shepherds?

130. Ezekiel 36　　　　　　　　　　　　　　　　　　<u>Test</u>: Ezekiel 21–33

   (a) For whose sake would God restore Israel?

131. Ezekiel 37

(a) What did God do to the valley of bones?

   (b) What did God's work among the bones symbolize?

   (c) Why did God tell Ezekiel to join two sticks together? What did it mean?

132. Ezekiel 38–39

   (a) Who would come from the north to attack peaceful Israel?

133. Ezekiel 40

134. Ezekiel 43

   (a) After the man showed Ezekiel the court and temple, what came from the east with the sound of many waters?

   (b) Why should Ezekiel describe the temple to the house of Israel?

135. Ezekiel 44

   (a) How had Israel profaned the temple?

136. Ezekiel 47–48

   (a) As they went east, what happened to the river flowing from the city?

137. Hosea 1:1—2:13 *Memorize* Hosea 4:1–6

   (a) What kind of wife did Hosea take?

   (b) What did Hosea name his first three children? What did the names mean? Why did he name them?

   (c) How were Hosea and Gomer like the LORD and Israel?

138. Hosea 2:14—3:5 <u>Test</u>: Ezekiel 34–48

   (a) After God punishes Israel for her sins, what will he do?

   (b) After Gomer left Hosea, what did Hosea do?

   (c) The people of Israel shall dwell many days without king or gods. What will they do in the latter days?

139. Hosea 4

   (a) Complete the statement: "My people are destroyed for ..."

   (b) God's contention was with whom?

140. Hosea 5:1—6:3

   (a) What did not permit the Israelites to return to their God?

141. Hosea 6:4—7:16

(a) What did God desire more than burnt offerings?

(b) How was Ephraim like a dove?

142. Hosea 8:1—9:9

(a) Israel sowed the wind. What did they reap?

143. Hosea 9:10—10:15

(a) What would happen to Ephraim's children?

(b) Israel should break up their fallow ground. Why?

(c) Israel should break up their fallow ground. What should she sow and reap?

144. Hosea 11–12

145. Hosea 13–14

(a) What causes Ephraim to be like the morning mist or like the dew that goes early away?

146. Joel 1

(a) Joel says, "Alas for the day." What day does he refer to?

(b) Why should the drunkards weep, the virgins lament, the farmers be ashamed, and the priests wail?

147. Joel 2 <u>Test</u>: Hosea

(a) What was the land like before God's army and after God's army?

(b) What could the people do to avoid the day of the LORD?

148. Joel 3 *Memorize* Amos 5:21–24

(a) Why were the nations gathered to the Valley of Jehoshaphat?

149. Amos 1–2

(a) List some nations with whom God was angry.

(b) What sins had Israel committed?

150. Amos 3–4 <u>Test</u>: Joel

(a) Complete the sentence, "Does disaster come to a city unless ... "

(b) God gave Israel lack of bread, withheld the rain, struck with blight and mildew, sent pestilence, and overthrew some. Yet ...

151. Amos 5

(a) What places should Israel not seek? Whom should they seek?

(b) List some things God hated.

(c) What did God want rolling like waters and streams?

152. Amos 6–7

(a) What were those at ease doing and not doing?

(b) When Amos saw the locusts and fire, what did he do?

153. Amos 8–9

(a) Why did some hope for the Sabbath's end?

(b) What kind of famine will God send upon Israel?

(c) After God shakes the house of Israel among the nations, what will he do?

154. Jonah 1–2   *Memorize* Jonah 4:10–11

(a) What did God command Jonah?

(b) What did Jonah do from the belly of the fish?

155. Jonah 3–4   <u>Test</u>: Amos

(a) How did Nineveh respond to Jonah's message?

(b) What lesson did God teach Jonah with the plant?

156. Micah 1–2

(a) The LORD is coming. The mountains will melt. The valley will split apart. Why?

(b) What were the powerful doing?

157. Micah 3–4

(a) How did the prophets' message differ between those who fed the prophets and those who didn't feed the prophets?

(b) What will happen in the latter days?

158. Micah 5–6

(a) Who will come from Bethlehem?

(b) What does the LORD require of you?

159. Nahum 1–2   *Memorize* Micah 6:6–8

(a) Whom will the LORD by no means clear?

160. Nahum 3   <u>Test</u>: Jonah and Micah

(a) When people hear about Nineveh's downfall, they will clap their hands. Why?

161. Habakkuk 1:1—2:5

    (a) What was Habakkuk's first complaint?

    (b) What was God's answer to Habakkuk's first complaint?

162. Habakkuk 2:6—3:19

    (a) What was Habakkuk's second complaint?

    (b) What was God's answer to Habakkuk's second complaint?

    (c) What did Habakkuk do after he heard God's answer to the second complaint?

163. Zephaniah 1–2

    (a) What will God do to the face of the earth?

    (b) What sinners in Judah does Zephaniah address?

    (c) What other nations would suffer God's wrath?

164. Zephaniah 3   Test: Nahum and Habakkuk

    (a) God will change the speech of the peoples. Why?

    (b) At the end of Zephaniah, what will God do for Zion?

165. Haggai 1–2

    (a) Why did the people lack food, drink, clothing, and money?

    (b) What did Zerubbabel, Joshua, and the people do after Haggai's words?

    (c) In glory, how shall the latter house compare with the former house?

166. Zechariah 1–2

    (a) The former prophets cried, "Return from your evil ways and your evil deeds." How did the peoples' fathers respond?

    (b) Why was the LORD upset with the nations at ease?

    (c) The people should flee from where to Zion?

167. Zechariah 3–4   Test: Zephaniah and Haggai

    (a) How was Joshua's clothing changed?

    (b) What was on either side of the golden lampstand?

    (c) To whom did God speak: "Not by might, nor by power, but by my Spirit."

168. Zechariah 7–8   *Memorize* Zechariah 8:14–17

    (a) The people fasted for themselves. What did God want?

    (b) God planned to help Jerusalem. What would the new Jerusalem be like?

169. Zechariah 9–10

    (a) What nations would suffer God's wrath?

    (b) How will Jerusalem's king come?

170. Zechariah 11

    (a) What kind of flock did the man shepherd?

    (b) What staffs were broken?

    (c) How much did they pay the shepherd?

171. Zechariah 12–13

    (a) The nations will come against Jerusalem. How will she fare?

    (b) Why will the inhabitants of Jerusalem weep bitterly?

    (c) On that day, what will happen to the prophets?

172. Malachi 1–2   <u>Test</u>: Zechariah

    (a) How had the priests despised God's name?

    (b) What was wrong with the priests' instruction?

    (c) Why didn't God favorably accept the peoples' offerings?

173. Malachi 3–4   <u>Test</u>: Malachi

    (a) Who will come before the LORD comes?

    (b) How did the people rob God?

13   Year Three Maps and Tests

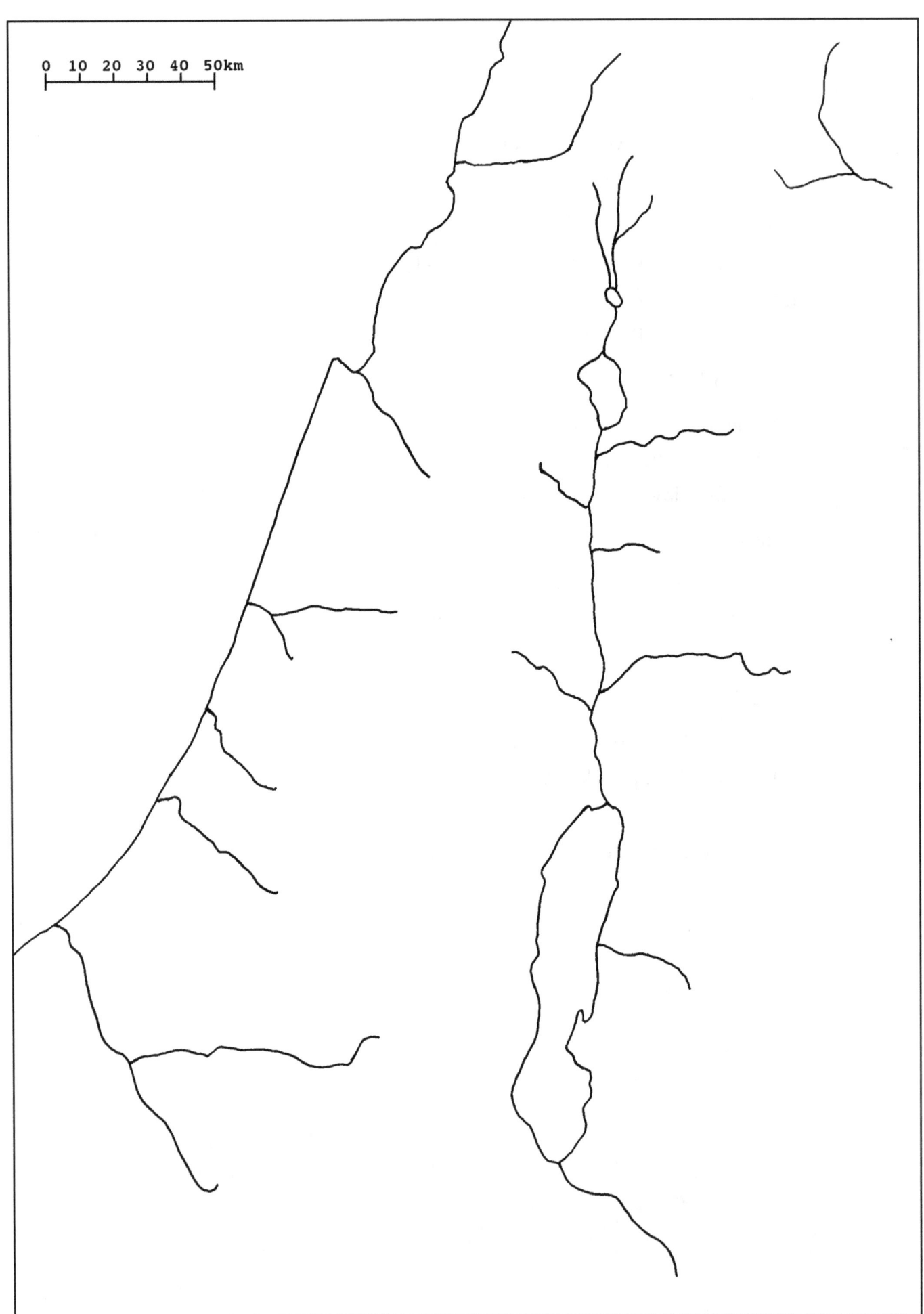

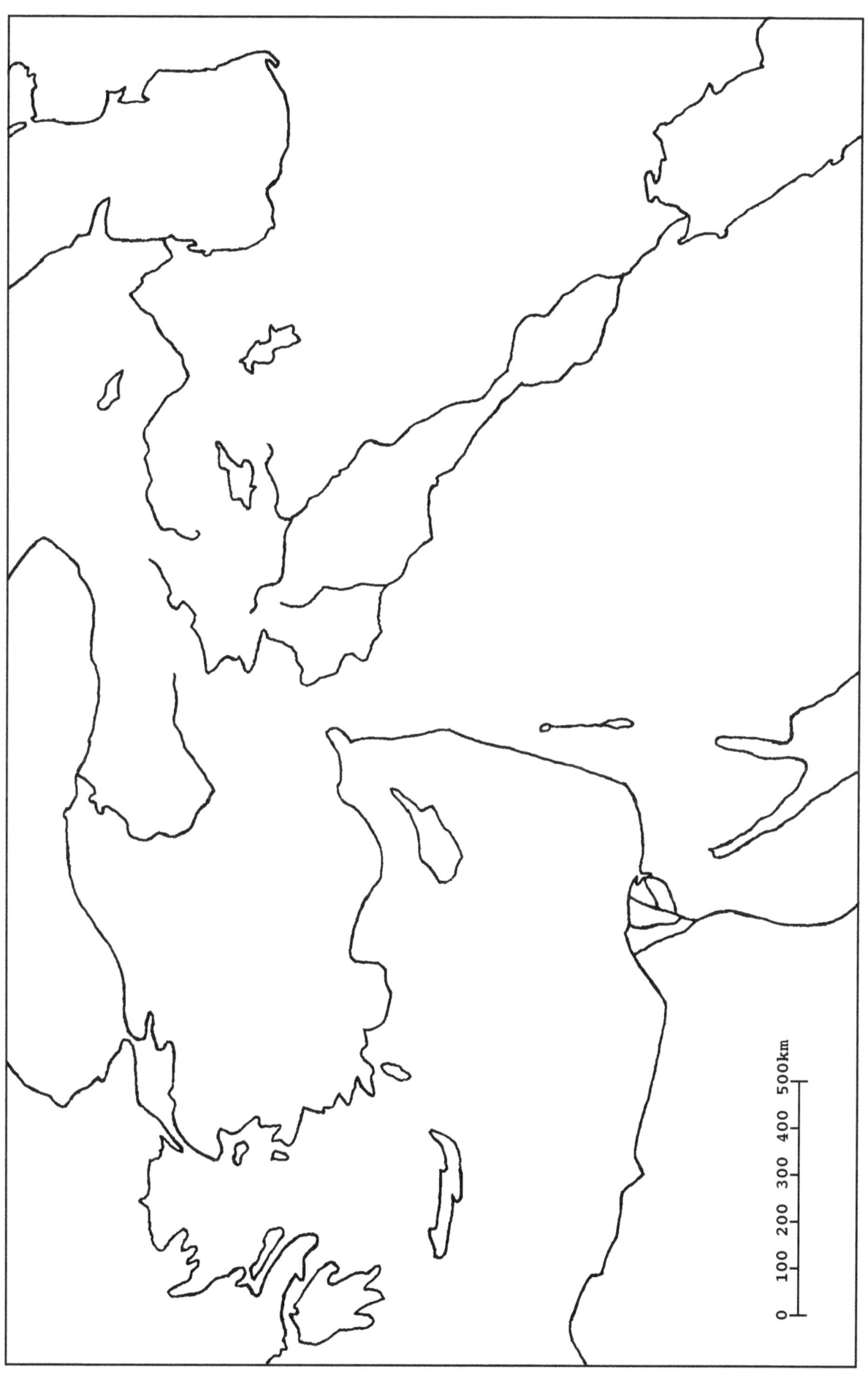

Esther

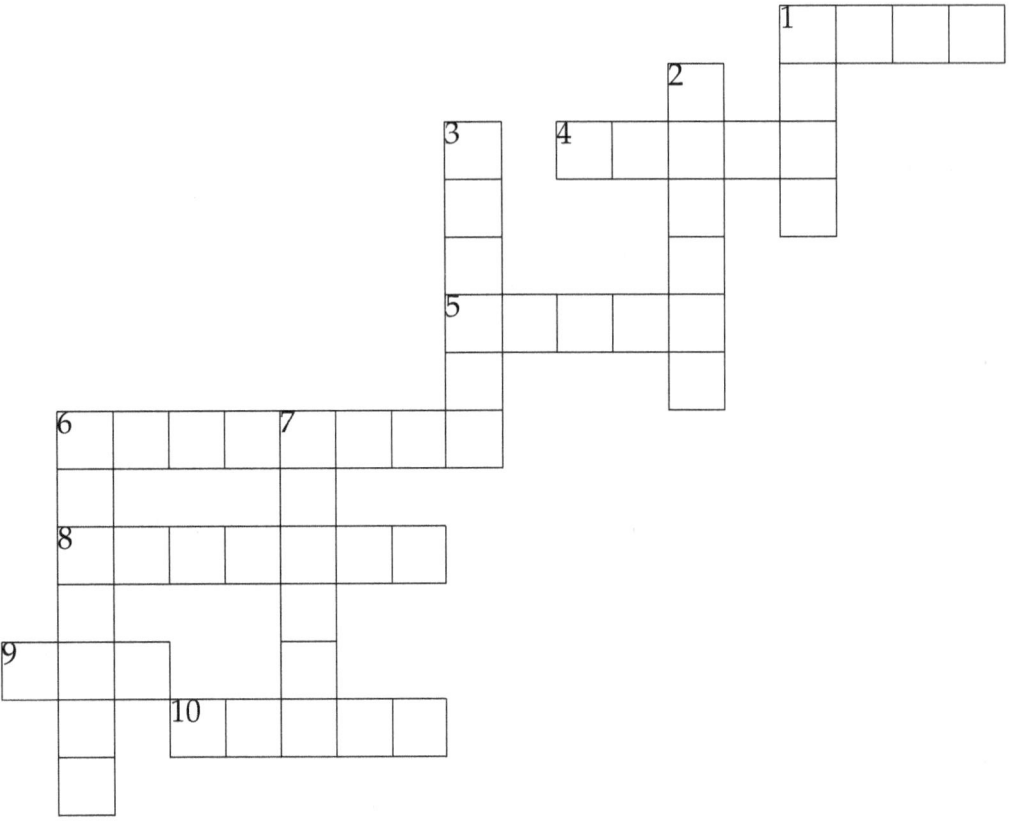

Across
1 Haman plotted to ____ the Jews.
4 Because of her actions Vashti was no longer ____.
5 After Esther exposed his plot, the king was angry with ____.
6 Ahasuerus honored ____.
8 Ahasuerus extended the golden ____ to Esther.
9 Esther's race.
10 Jews celebrate ____, remembering the events in Esther.

Down
1 Esther planned to plead with the ____ on behalf of the Jews.
2 When the Jews heard they could ____ themselves, they celebrated.
3 Queen ____ upset Ahasuerus.
6 The Jews gained ____ on the 13th day of the 12th month.
7 ____ pleased Ahasuerus more than the other women.

Job 1–10

Directions: Circle the letter of the best answer.

1. What kind of man was Job?

    (a) blameless and upright

    (b) wicked

    (c) poor

    (d) depressed

2. Why did Satan think Job feared God?

    (a) because Job believed in God's greatness

    (b) because Job was told he should

    (c) because fear brought God's blessing

    (d) because God punished Job before

3. How did Satan harm Job the second time?

    (a) destroyed his cattle

    (b) struck him with bodily sores

    (c) killed his sons and daughters

    (d) kidnapped his wife

4. After Job was harmed, how did he act toward God?

    (a) He did not sin with his lips.

    (b) He cursed God.

    (c) He praised God for striking him.

    (d) He offered gifts to God.

5. Who came to comfort Job?

    (a) his wife

    (b) three friends

    (c) his children

    (d) the king

6. What did Job wish about his birth?

    (a) He was born in happier times.

    (b) He was born in Egypt.

    (c) He wasn't deformed.

    (d) It never happened.

Job 11–42

What did Job's three friends believe about Job? Why did Job disagree?

When God spoke, he asked questions. List at least three of them.

How did Job react to God's questions?

How did God treat Job after their encounter?

Proverbs 1–9

Directions: Fill in the blanks.

1. _____ wrote Proverbs.

2. The Proverbs were written to know _____ and instruction.

3. The Proverbs were written to receive instruction in wise dealing, in _____, justice and equity.

4. The fear of the Lord is the beginning of _____.

5. If you seek wisdom and understanding, then you will understand the _____ of the Lord and find the knowledge of God.

6. Trust in the _____ with all your heart, and do not lean on your own understanding.

7. Solomon says, "Keep your way from her, and do not go near the door of her house." He's speaking about a forbidden _____.

Proverbs 10–31

Explain these Proverbs in your own words. Look each one up.

Proverbs 10:19

Proverbs 16:32

Proverbs 21:13

Ecclesiastes

Directions: Circle the letter of the best answer.

1. When the preacher observed things in the world, he said,

    (a) "All is beautiful."

    (b) "All is evil."

    (c) "All is vanity."

    (d) "All is good."

2. The preacher gained wisdom. He found in much wisdom is much

    (a) sorrow

    (b) power

    (c) joy

    (d) weariness

3. When you toil, your work goes to someone else after you die. What's wrong with that?

    (a) He will waste it.

    (b) Who knows whether he is wise or foolish.

    (c) You should enjoy it longer.

    (d) Nothing.

4. Name some things for which there is a time.

    (a) birth and death

    (b) mourn and dance

    (c) weep and laugh

    (d) all of the above

5. There is nothing better for man than to

    (a) live for himself

    (b) live expecting it is the last day

    (c) be joyful and to do good

    (d) be purposed and disciplined

6. Why are two better than one?

    (a) If one falls, one will lift him up.

    (b) If they lie together, they keep warm.

    (c) A man may prevail against one alone but not two together.

    (d) All of the above

7. Why should you not be hasty to speak to God?

    (a) God lacks time for mortals.

    (b) God is in heaven and you are on earth.

    (c) God despises man.

    (d) All of the above

8. Who is better off than a man who lives long but remains unsatisfied and has an improper burial?

    (a) a stillborn child

    (b) a king

    (c) a poor man

    (d) a donkey

9. Solomon saw a vanity: a righteous man who perishes but a wicked man who

    (a) receives praise
    (b) gathers wealth
    (c) prolongs his life
    (d) becomes king

10. What person should a man enjoy life with?

    (a) his children
    (b) his wife
    (c) his mother
    (d) all of the above

11. After the poor, wise man delivered the city, how was he treated?

    (a) He was honored.
    (b) He was made king.
    (c) He was thanked.
    (d) He was not remembered.

12. As you do not know the way the spirit comes to bones in the womb, so you do not know

    (a) the work of God
    (b) the way to choose a wife
    (c) what is right or wrong
    (d) what is in a man's heart

13. What should you remember in your youth?

    (a) your father
    (b) the way of life
    (c) your creator
    (d) your teacher

14. What is the end of the matter?

    (a) Store treasures on earth.
    (b) Live for yourself.
    (c) Fear God and keep his commandments.
    (d) Seek wisdom, pleasure and toil.

Song of Solomon

Directions: Fill in the blanks.

1. Song of Solomon's two main characters are _____ and his _____

2. Solomon's bride had _____ skin.

3. "I adjure you, O daughters of Jerusalem, that you not stir up or awaken _____ until it pleases."

4. "His head is the finest gold; his locks are wavy, _____ as a raven."

5. "His arms are rods of _____, set with jewels."

6. "Your hair is like a flock of _____ leaping down the slopes of Gilead."

7. "Your teeth are like a flock of _____ that have come up from the washing."

8. Love is as strong as _____.

Isaiah 1–7

In Isaiah 1, Isaiah compares Judah to a human body. How was Judah like a human body?

In Isaiah 5, Isaiah compares Judah to a vineyard. Describe the vineyard metaphor.

In Isaiah 6, Isaiah has a vision of God. Describe the vision.

Isaiah 8–23

```
P  E  O  P  L  E  Z  O
O  U  N  O  B  V  N  R
H  B  R  M  I  E  P  L
Y  D  D  E  N  R  U  B
H  S  M  O  C  L  V  Q
B  B  P  V  V  A  S  L
L  B  T  I  V  S  Y  L
I  B  E  L  R  T  W  C
J  O  Q  A  C  I  T  F
I  X  N  T  Y  N  T  Q
D  E  H  H  O  G  F  D
O  U  X  P  K  D  Z  O
C  T  G  A  T  E  B  F
G  W  G  N  Z  J  I  S
```

1. Isaiah should fear the __ __ __ __.

2. Zebulun and __ __ __ __ __ __ __ __ would see a great light.

3. He shall be called Wonderful Counselor, Mighty God,

   __ __ __ __ __ __ __ __ __ __ Father.

4. The warrior's clothing will be __ __ __ __ __ __.

5. Assyria's pride over God was like an __ __ __ boasting over a woodcutter.

6. A __ __ __ __ __ __ of wisdom and understanding shall rest on the shoot of Jesse.

7. After God punishes Babylon, there will be few __ __ __ __ __ __.

Isaiah 24–33

Directions: Circle the letter of the best answer.

1. What will the LORD do to the earth?

    (a) He will burn it and consume it.
    (b) He will empty it and make it desolate.
    (c) He will plant it with new trees.
    (d) He will fill it with beauty.

2. What will the people in the west and east do?

    (a) give glory to the LORD
    (b) save the unrighteous
    (c) commit transgression
    (d) pray continually

3. What will God swallow up on the mountain of the LORD?

    (a) the wicked
    (b) rotten trees
    (c) the rain
    (d) death

4. Complete the sentence, "If favor is shown to the wicked, he does not learn ___."

    (a) fear
    (b) wickedness
    (c) righteousness
    (d) knowledge

5. What did God's words sound like to those who would not hear?

    (a) a strange language
    (b) precept upon precept
    (c) hatred
    (d) a thunderclap

6. God will lay a cornerstone in Zion. What will justice and righteousness be like?

    (a) berries and refreshment
    (b) a king and prince
    (c) bread and water
    (d) a line and plumb line

7. People drew near to God with their mouths and honored him with their lips. What was wrong?

    (a) Their hearts were far from God.
    (b) Nothing.
    (c) They didn't study the Bible.
    (d) Their children didn't honor God.

8. From what nation did people seek help?

    (a) Syria
    (b) Philistia
    (c) Egypt
    (d) Moab

9. Isaiah prophesied destruction to the fields and cities to which women?

   (a) the complacent

   (b) the selfish

   (c) the witches

   (d) the God-haters

10. Who can dwell with the consuming fire?

   (a) the warrior

   (b) the tried and tested

   (c) the righteous and upright

   (d) the priest

Isaiah 34–42

Briefly tell the story of Sennacherib and Jerusalem.

_____

_____

_____

_____

_____

_____

_____

_____

_____

What kind of God is the LORD? List some of his traits.

_____

_____

_____

_____

_____

_____

_____

_____

Isaiah 43–55

Across

1 The mountains may depart, but God's steadfast _____ shall not depart.
5 The servant was wounded for our _____.
9 Even though a woman may _____ her nursing child, God will not _____ Zion.
11 The daughter of the Chaldeans said in her heart, "I am, and there is no one _____ me."

Down

1 Not only would the servant restore Israel, he would be a _____ for the nations.
2 After the servant _____, he will rise again.
3 Those who know righteousness should not fear _____.
4 Widowhood and loss of _____ will come upon the daughter of the Chaldeans.
6 God's word that goes from his mouth shall not return _____.
7 God says, "Turn to me and be _____, all the ends of the earth."
8 Those who fear the LORD should _____ in the name of the LORD and rely on his God.
10 _____ declared things to come long ago.

Isaiah 56–66

Directions: Fill in the blanks.

1. God would not separate from his people the foreigners who _____ themselves to the LORD.

2. Some _____ people perish to be spared from calamity.

3. People sought their own pleasure when they _____; therefore, God did not acknowledge it.

4. God wanted a fast that _____ the oppressed and cared for the needy.

5. God did not hear their _____, because sin separated them from God.

6. God was displeased that there was no _____.

7. "Arise, shine, for your _____ has come, and the glory of the LORD has risen upon you."

8. The sun won't be needed for light, because _____ will be your everlasting light.

9. The _____ of the LORD was upon him to bring good news to the poor, to bind up the brokenhearted, and to proclaim liberty to the captives.

10. God's garments were red after trodding the _____ alone.

11. The people were unclean, and their _____ deeds were like a polluted garment.

12. God spread out his hands all day to a _____ people.

13. God will create new _____ and a new earth.

14. God will look upon he who is humble and contrite in spirit and _____ at his word.

Lamentations

Summarize Lamentations. Use at least five sentences. Include the major concepts.

Ezekiel 1–11

```
T N G D T K W M H A I R Y T
J R J B V F I T B O E W G D
U F L E S H V K E B A M P N
A B Z G R F Q S E U C F O Q
A K D F C U P L I R Y N P L
T B C E Y E S P A N T P G T
I A O C X L M A F E O V B M
R N A I I J T E L D E D Z R
I H L D D E Y V Q E H R J T
P E S N O I T A N I M O B A
S Z O C L U U O E G S L N T
R E H F S V P K T R X X O G
```

1. Ezekiel saw four living creatures with wheels underneath. The wheel rims were full of __ __ __ __.

2. Above the creatures was an expanse, and above the expanse was a throne. The __ __ __ __ sat on the throne.

3. God called Israel a house of __ __ __ __ __ __.

4. Ezekiel built a model of __ __ __ __ __ __ __ __ __ to play-act its siege.

5. Ezekiel took his __ __ __ __ and separated it into three parts.

6. He __ __ __ __ __ __ part of it, struck part of it, and scattered part of it to symbolize God's judgment on Jerusalem.

7. When God strikes Israel, the slain bodies will lie before their __ __ __ __ __.

269

8. The _ _ _ _ _ _ lifted Ezekiel up and brought him to Jerusalem.

9. God showed Ezekiel _ _ _ _ _ _ _ _ _ _ _ in Jerusalem.

10. The man clothed in linen scattered _ _ _ _ _ over the city.

11. Those in Jerusalem thought the land was for them and the

    _ _ _ _ _ _ were far from the LORD.

12. God would give the exiles a heart of _ _ _ _ _ when they returned.

Ezekiel 12–20

Directions: Circle the letter of the best answer.

1. Why did Ezekiel prepare an exile's baggage and go into exile by day?

    (a) He was symbolizing what would happen to those in Jerusalem.

    (b) Nebuchadnezzar wanted to move the exiles from the Chebar canal.

    (c) He wanted to visit Jerusalem.

    (d) The exiles wanted him to leave.

2. The people said, "The days grow long, and every vision comes to nothing." What did God say?

    (a) The visions come to nothing because of your sin.

    (b) Soon I will restore you.

    (c) The days are near, and the fulfillment of every vision.

    (d) Be patient; my days are longer than your days.

3. The false prophets claimed their words came from ____.

    (a) Zedekiah

    (b) God

    (c) themselves

    (d) Nebuchadnezzar

4. Some worshipped idols yet inquired of God. What did God say?

    (a) He wouldn't answer them, because they sinned.

    (b) He wouldn't answer them, because they had the written word of God.

    (c) He would answer them, because they were turning toward him.

    (d) He would answer them by cutting them off.

5. When a land sins against the LORD, if Noah, Daniel and Job were in it, who could they save?

    (a) only themselves

    (b) their families and themselves

    (c) the cities where they live and themselves

    (d) the whole land

6. Israel was like a woman. How did God *not* care for her?

    (a) He made her flourish like a plant of the field.

    (b) He adorned her with ornaments and bracelets.

    (c) He gave her beautiful horses.

    (d) He spread his garment over her.

7. Israel was like a woman. How did she *not* respond to God's help?

   (a) She took God's jewels and made idols.
   (b) She remained faithful to the Lord.
   (c) She whored after other men.
   (d) She sacrificed her children to idols.

8. An eagle planted a twig. How did the twig grow?

   (a) It grew straight up.
   (b) It died.
   (c) It grew toward the eagle.
   (d) It bent its roots and shot its branches toward another eagle.

9. How was Zedekiah like the twig?

   (a) He would soon die.
   (b) He abided in the Lord.
   (c) He was planted by Nebuchadnezzar but turned toward Pharaoh.
   (d) He despised everyone's help.

10. What was wrong with the proverb, "The fathers have eaten sour grapes, and the children's teeth are set on edge."?

    (a) The soul who sins shall die.
    (b) The children's teeth were straight.
    (c) Nothing.
    (d) The mothers were excluded.

11. The Lord has no pleasure in the death of anyone. He wants people to ___.

    (a) stay the same and live
    (b) repent and live
    (c) have faith and live
    (d) worship and live

12. What was in Israel's mind, but it would never happen?

    (a) The Lord would restore them.
    (b) They would live righteously.
    (c) They would return to the land.
    (d) They would be like the other nations, worshipping idols.

Ezekiel 21–33

Briefly tell the story of Oholah and Oholibah. Use at least five sentences.

Choose two nations that surrounded Israel. What did God plan for them, and why?

Ezekiel 34–48

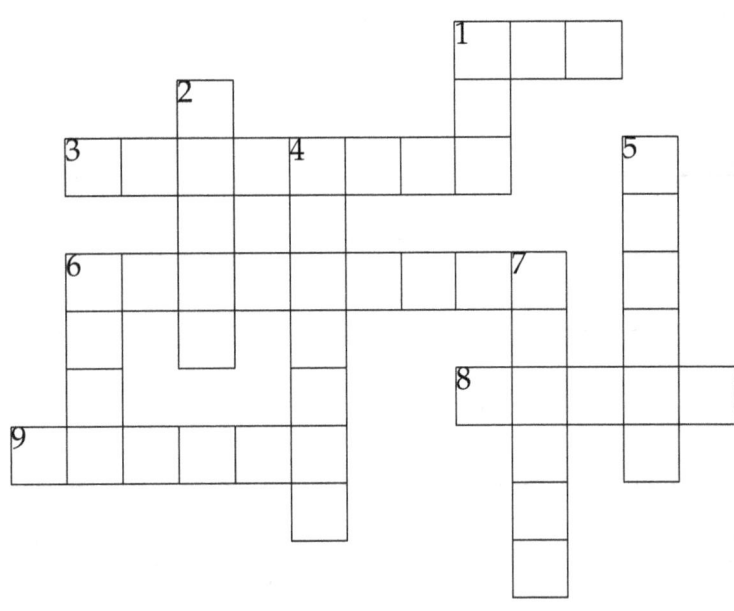

Across

1 _____ will come from the north and attack peaceful Israel.
3 Israel _____ the temple by allowing uncircumcised foreigners in it.
6 The _____ did not feed or seek the flock.
8 As they went east, the _____ became deeper.
9 The man like bronze showed Ezekiel the court and _____.

Down

1 _____ will search for his sheep and seek them out.
2 Skin, flesh and breath came upon the dry _____.
4 God told Ezekiel to describe the temple so Israel will be _____ of their iniquities.
5 God will open Israel's _____ and bring them up from them.
6 God will restore Israel for his own _____.
7 Ezekiel joined two _____ together to show Israel and Judah will be combined.

Hosea

Directions: Fill in the blanks.

1. Hosea took a wife of _____.

2. Hosea's three children were named _____, _____, and _____.

3. Hosea's relationship with Gomer was like the Lord's relationship with _____.

4. After God punishes Israel for her sins, he will _____ her.

5. After Gomer left Hosea, Hosea _____ her back.

6. The people of Israel shall dwell many days without king or gods. In the latter days, they will return and _____ the Lord their God.

7. "My people are destroyed for lack of _____."

8. God's contention was with Israel's _____.

9. Israel's _____ did not permit them to return to their God.

10. "For I desire _____ _____ and not sacrifice, the knowledge of God rather than burnt offerings."

11. "Ephraim is like a _____, silly and without sense, calling to Egypt, going to Assyria."

12. "For they sow the wind, and they shall reap the _____."

13. God will bereave Ephraim of her _____.

14. "Sow for yourselves _____;

    reap _____; break up your fallow ground, for it

    is time to _____ the LORD that he may come and rain righteousness upon

    you."

15. The more God called Israel, the more they went _____.

16. Despite her sins, God could not give up _____.

17. Ephraim's idols made her like the morning _____.

Joel

Joel says, "Alas for the day!" What day does he refer to? What things will happen on that day? Why will they happen? How could it be avoided?

Amos

```
R C K D E T N E L E R M Z F B R
O F Z E J E R X C G J H K A Y I
O J M G V Y U C D B U N R U Z G
P E P E F A T K X L S E D M T H
D H I L S Z E M M L T E W T V T
T R A N S G R E S S I O N S T E
G B V J A P N T A H C X Q A N O
Q D O S P T K S K G E C N B B U
Q D E Z R E I E M R S M A B I S
O E E T A D G O K E N I M A F V
K V N A A M Z Z N P O D D T M G
U S E K A H S O J S T L X H R Z
```

1. Amos begins with God's judgment on Israel's surrounding _ _ _ _ _ _ _.

2. "For three _ _ _ _ _ _ _ _ _ _ _ _ of Israel, and for four, I will not revoke the punishment."

3. Israel sold the _ _ _ _ _ _ _ _ _ for silver.

4. Israel trampled the head of the _ _ _ _ into the dust of the earth.

5. "Does _ _ _ _ _ _ _ _ come to a city unless the LORD has done it?"

6. To Israel, God gave lack of bread, withheld the rain, struck with blight and mildew, sent pestilence, and overthrew, yet they did not _ _ _ _ _ _ to him.

7. "_ _ _ _ the LORD and live, lest he break out like fire in the house of Joseph."

8. God _ _ _ _ _ Israel's feasts, offerings, and songs.

9. "But let ___ ___ ___ ___ ___ ___ ___ roll down like waters, and righteousness like an ever-flowing stream."

10. Those at ease lay on beds of ivory, ate lambs, sang songs, and drank wine, but did not ___ ___ ___ ___ ___ ___ over the ruin of Joseph.

11. When Amos saw the locusts and fire, he pleaded with God to forgive and cease, and God ___ ___ ___ ___ ___ ___ ___ ___.

12. Some hoped for the end of the ___ ___ ___ ___ ___ ___ ___, so they could cheat and buy the poor for silver and the needy for sandals.

13. The days are coming, when God will send a ___ ___ ___ ___ ___ ___ of hearing the word of the Lord.

14. After God ___ ___ ___ ___ ___ ___ the house of Israel among the nations, he will raise up, repair, and rebuild the booth of David.

Jonah and Micah

Directions: Circle the letter of the best answer.

1. God commanded Jonah to
   (a) go to Nineveh and call out against it.
   (b) preach against Jerusalem.
   (c) wear a yoke.
   (d) lead an army against Assyria.

2. From the belly of the fish, Jonah
   (a) died.
   (b) cried.
   (c) prayed.
   (d) slept.

3. How did Nineveh respond to Jonah's message?
   (a) They didn't listen.
   (b) They repented.
   (c) They stoned Jonah.
   (d) They imprisoned Jonah.

4. What lesson did God teach Jonah with the plant?
   (a) God pities the lost.
   (b) God hates evil.
   (c) God creates.
   (d) God destroys.

5. Why will the mountains melt and the valleys split open at the LORD's coming?
   (a) God is powerful.
   (b) God plans destruction.
   (c) The Assyrians will be destroyed.
   (d) Israel transgressed.

6. What were the powerful doing?
   (a) seizing fields
   (b) stripping robes from those who pass by
   (c) driving women from their houses
   (d) all of the above

7. The prophets cried ___ when someone gave them something to eat, but they declared war against those who didn't feed them.
   (a) plenty
   (b) blessing
   (c) peace
   (d) destruction

8. What will happen in the latter days?
   (a) The world will be destroyed.
   (b) The LORD's mountain shall be the highest.
   (c) David's line will cease.
   (d) Jerusalem's water supply shall cease.

9. A ruler in Israel will come from where?
   (a) Bethlehem
   (b) Samaria
   (c) Jerusalem
   (d) Tirzah

10. What does the Lord require of you?

   (a) to sacrifice burnt offerings
   (b) to build altars
   (c) to give away your children
   (d) to do justice, to love kindness, and to walk humbly with God

Nahum and Habakkuk

Answer in complete sentences.

1. Whom will the LORD by no means clear?

2. When people hear about Nineveh's downfall, they will clap their hands. Why?

3. What was Habakkuk's first complaint?

4. What was God's answer to Habakkuk's first complaint?

5. What was Habakkuk's second complaint?

6. What was God's answer to Habakkuk's second complaint?

7. What did Habakkuk do after he heard God's second answer?

Zephaniah and Haggai

Directions: Fill in the blanks.

1. God will utterly sweep away _____ from the face of the earth.

2. Zephaniah addresses the sinners who _____ to the LORD and yet _____ by Milcom.

3. Not only Judah, but _____ and _____ would suffer God's wrath.

4. In a later time, all _____ will call upon the name of the LORD.

5. At the end of Zephaniah, God will rejoice and exult over _____.

6. In Haggai, the people lacked food, drink, clothing and money because they had not built the _____.

7. After hearing Haggai's words, _____, Joshua and the people began constructing the temple.

8. The latter house shall be _____ than the former house in glory.

Zechariah

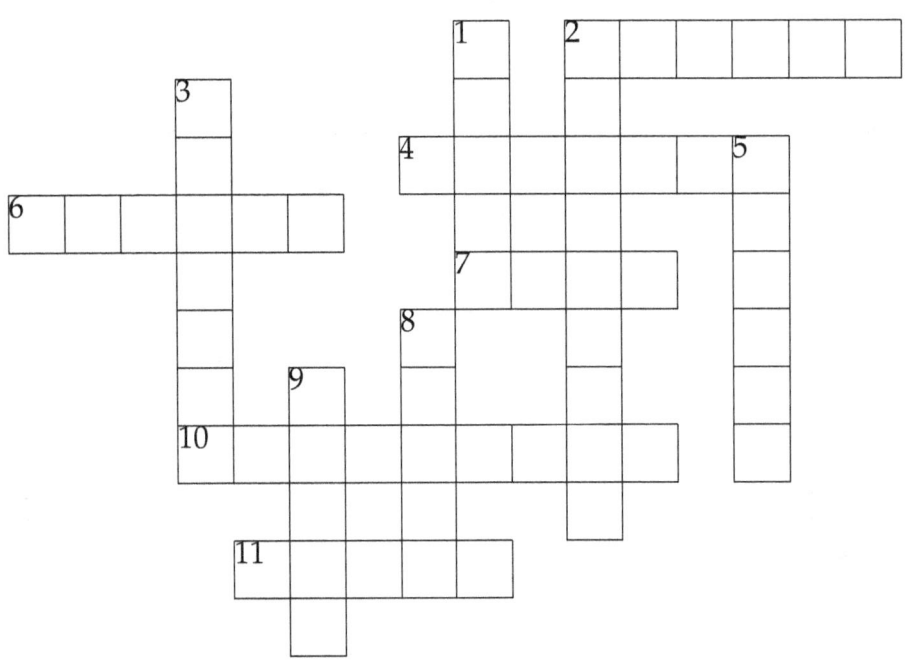

Across

2 They clothed ____ with clean garments.
4 The people of Jerusalem shall weep bitterly for the one they ____.
6 The people ____ for themselves, but God wanted truth, kindness, and mercy.
7 The LORD was angry with the nations at ____.
10 He shepherded the flock doomed to ____.
11 Flee from the land of the ____.

Down

1 ____ trees were on the right and left of the lampstand.
2 ____ shall have streets full of boys and girls playing.
3 God said, "Return," but the ____ did not listen.
5 Jerusalem's king shall come mounted on a ____.
8 God told Zerubbabel, "Not by ____, nor by power, but by my Spirit."
9 The shepherd broke the staffs of ____ and Union.

Malachi

Malachi describes four major sins of the priests and people. Choose two of them and write a paragraph about each. Explain the sin and, if applicable, the bad thinking behind the sin, and the consequences of the sin.

Part VI

Year Four
(Matthew through Revelation)

14 Year Four Plan

1. Luke 1:1–38 *Memorize* Matthew 3:1–6

    (a) Who appeared to Zechariah in the temple?

    (b) What did Gabriel tell Zechariah?

    (c) What did Gabriel tell Mary?

2. Luke 1:39–80

    (a) What did Elizabeth's baby do when Elizabeth heard Mary's greeting?

    (b) What happened after Zechariah wrote, "His name is John"?

    (c) What did Zechariah prophesy his son would do?

3. Matthew 1

    (a) Matthew begins with whose genealogy?

    (b) Joseph planned to divorce Mary. Why didn't he?

4. Luke 2:1–40

    (a) Why were Joseph and Mary in Bethlehem?

    (b) To whom did the angels announce Jesus' birth?

    (c) How did Simeon and Anna act when they saw the child?

5. Luke 2:41–52, Matthew 2

    (a) When Jesus' parents found him, they asked, "Why have you treated us so?" How did Jesus respond?

    (b) Who came from the east, following a star?

    (c) How was Jesus saved from Herod's slaughter?

6. Matthew 3

    (a) What did John the Baptist preach?

    (b) What happened immediately after Jesus was baptized?

7. Matthew 4 <u>Test</u>: Matthew 1–2, Luke 1–2

    (a) The devil tempted Jesus with three temptations. What were they?

    (b) How did Jesus respond to the devil's temptations?

    (c) Jesus went throughout Galilee doing what?

8. Matthew 5 *Memorize* Matthew 5:43–48

    (a) In the Sermon on the Mount, name some groups that are blessed.

(b) Jesus did not come to abolish the Law and Prophets. What did he come to do?

(c) Jesus taught about anger, lust, divorce, oaths, retaliation, and love. Choose one. What was said about it; what did Jesus teach about it?

9. Matthew 6

    (a) How should giving, prayer, and fasting be done before others?

    (b) Where should you store treasure?

    (c) You should not be anxious about your life. What should you seek?

10. Matthew 7

    (a) What principle did Jesus teach with the "specks and logs" picture?

    (b) What sums up the Law and the Prophets?

    (c) How can you recognize a false prophet?

    (d) What principle did Jesus teach with the "house on rock and house on sand" picture?

11. Matthew 8

    (a) What amazed Jesus about the centurion?

    (b) What did Jesus do about the great storm?

12. Matthew 9   Test: Matthew 3–7

    (a) What statement to the paralytic upset the scribes?

    (b) What did Jesus do for the ruler's daughter?

13. Matthew 10

    (a) Jesus sent out the twelve disciples. What instructions did he give them?

    (b) Jesus said, "I am sending you as sheep among wolves." What did he predict men would do?

    (c) Jesus said, "I have not come to bring peace, but a sword." Who is not worthy of Jesus?

14. Matthew 11

    (a) John wondered if Jesus was the one. How did Jesus respond?

    (b) How great was John?

    (c) Why did Jesus say woe to Chorazin, Bethsaida and Capernaum?

15. Matthew 12:1–37   Test: Matthew 8–10

    (a) Jesus' disciples plucked grain on the Sabbath and upset the Pharisees. How did Jesus respond?

(b) The Pharisees believed Jesus cast out demons by Beelzebul. How did Jesus respond?

16. Matthew 12:38—13:23 *Memorize* The Twelve Disciples

    (a) Why will the men of Nineveh and the queen of the south condemn Jesus' generation?

    (b) List the four places where the sower's seed fell.

    (c) In the parable of the sower, what did the good soil represent?

17. Matthew 13:24–58

    (a) In the parable of the weeds, who are the weeds?

    (b) How is a prophet treated in his hometown?

18. Matthew 14

    (a) Why did Herod behead John the Baptist?

    (b) The disciples wanted a crowd to go away and get food. What did Jesus do?

    (c) Peter walked on the water with Jesus. Why did he start sinking?

19. Matthew 15 *Memorize* Matthew 16:24–28

    (a) The Pharisees broke God's commandment for what?

    (b) What defiles a person?

20. Matthew 16 Test: Matthew 11–14

    (a) Jesus said, "Who do you say that I am?" How did Peter reply?

    (b) If you would come after Jesus, what must you do?

21. Matthew 17

    (a) Jesus took Peter, James, and John up a high mountain. What did they see?

    (b) Jesus said Elijah has already come. Of whom was he speaking?

22. Matthew 18

    (a) Who is the greatest in the kingdom of heaven?

    (b) How many times should you forgive a brother who sins against you?

    (c) Jesus told a story of a king and debtors. Why should you forgive your brother from your heart?

23. Luke 15

    (a) There is joy in heaven over a sinner who does what?

(b) What did the prodigal do with his share of the property?

(c) When the prodigal returned, how did his father greet him?

24. Luke 16

    (a) Why did the master commend the dishonest manager?

    (b) If people do not hear whom, then neither will they be convinced if someone should rise from the dead?

25. Matthew 19

    (a) The rich man asked, "What must I do to have eternal life?" What did he lack?

    (b) What is easier than a rich man entering the kingdom of God?

26. Matthew 20 <u>Test</u>: Matthew 15–18

    (a) The master paid each laborer a denarius. Why did some grumble?

    (b) The mother of James and John wanted her sons to sit on Jesus' right and left. How is someone great among Jesus' disciples?

27. Matthew 21 *Memorize* Matthew 27:32–50

    (a) As Jesus entered Jerusalem, what did the crowds shout?

    (b) Why did Jesus overturn the money-changers' tables?

    (c) What did the tenants do to the vineyard owner's son?

28. Matthew 22

    (a) Someone asked, "Is it lawful to pay taxes to Caesar?" How did Jesus respond?

    (b) What is the greatest commandment in the law?

29. Matthew 23

    (a) List at least three things the Pharisees had done wrong.

    (b) What will the scribes and Pharisees do to the prophets, wise men, and scribes Jesus sends them?

30. Matthew 24 <u>Test</u>: Matthew 19–22

    (a) List some signs of the end of the age.

    (b) If someone said, "Jesus returned," how could you test his claim?

    (c) How can you be ready for Christ's return?

31. Matthew 25

    (a) Why were some virgins excluded from the marriage feast?

(b) Why were two servants commended in the parable of the talents?

(c) What was the difference between the sheep and the goats?

32. Matthew 26:1–35

    (a) The disciples thought a woman's act was wasteful. What had she done?

    (b) What did the bread and wine mean?

33. Matthew 26:36–75 <u>Test</u>: Matthew 23–25

    (a) What was Jesus doing in Gethsemane before he was captured?

    (b) With what did Judas betray Jesus?

    (c) Why did the scribes and Council put Jesus on trial?

    (d) When a servant girl said Peter was with Jesus, how did Peter respond?

34. Matthew 27:1–31

    (a) How did Judas's life end?

    (b) Pilate gave the crowd a choice: which prisoner shall be released? Whom did they choose?

    (c) Why did Pilate wash his hands in front of the crowd?

35. Matthew 27:32–66

    (a) How did the passers-by, the chief priests, the scribes, and the elders treat Jesus while he was on the cross?

    (b) What occurred immediately after Jesus' death?

    (c) How did the chief priests secure the tomb?

36. Matthew 28

    (a) What did Mary Magdalene and Mary find at the tomb?

    (b) What did the angel tell the women?

    (c) In Matthew, what final command did Jesus give the disciples?

37. Luke 24

    (a) What did Jesus teach the men travelling to Emmaus?

    (b) How did the disciples know Jesus wasn't just a spirit?

38. Acts 1 <u>Test</u>: Matthew 26–28

    (a) How did Jesus leave earth?

    (b) Who replaced Judas?

39. Acts 2

    (a) How did the Holy Spirit come at Pentecost?

    (b) According to Peter what had God done to Jesus, and what had the people done to Jesus?

40. Acts 3

    (a) What did Peter and John give the lame man at the Beautiful Gate?

    (b) By what power did Peter and John heal the lame man?

41. Acts 4

    (a) The high priest and elders commanded Peter and John not to speak in the name of Jesus anymore. How did Peter and John reply?

    (b) After Peter and John were released, for what did the believers pray?

42. Acts 5

    (a) Why did Ananias and Sapphira die?

    (b) Why did people bring the sick to the apostles?

    (c) Gamaliel convinced the council not to murder the apostles. What did he say?

43. Acts 6–7 *Memorize* Acts 1:6–8

    (a) Why did the disciples choose seven men to serve?

    (b) Why was Stephen brought before the council?

    (c) How did God's actions toward Joseph and Moses differ from the Israelites' actions?

    (d) Stephen called the rulers stiff-necked, because they always resisted what?

44. Acts 8 <u>Test</u>: Acts 1–5

    (a) As the persecution began, what did the believers do?

    (b) Why did Peter rebuke Simon in Samaria?

    (c) What did Philip do for the Ethiopian?

45. Acts 9

    (a) What happened to Saul on the road to Damascus?

    (b) In Damascus, what did Saul say about Jesus in the synagogues?

46. Acts 10

    (a) What kind of man was Cornelius?

    (b) Describe Peter's vision in Joppa.

(c) What happened as Peter spoke to Cornelius's household?

47. Acts 11:19—12:25

    (a) How was Peter rescued from prison?

    (b) How did Herod die?

48. Acts 13   <u>Test</u>: Acts 6–10

    (a) What was wrong with Bar-Jesus, the magician in Cyprus?

    (b) Who spoke to the crowd in Antioch in Pisidia?

    (c) How did the Jews in Antioch in Pisidia respond to Paul's message?

49. Acts 14

    (a) After a lame man walked, how did the people of Lystra treat Barnabas and Paul?

    (b) As they returned to Lystra, Iconium, and Antioch, what did Barnabas and Paul do?

50. Acts 15

    (a) What were some in Judea teaching the brothers in Antioch? It bothered them greatly.

    (b) What did the apostles and elders in Jerusalem decide about circumcision?

    (c) How did the Jerusalem leaders make their decision known?

51. Acts 16   *Memorize* Acts 17:22–31

    (a) Paul and Silas took another man with them in Lystra. What was his name?

    (b) Why were Paul and Silas imprisoned in Philippi?

    (c) What happened at midnight in the Philippian jail?

52. Acts 17   <u>Test</u>: Acts 11–15

    (a) Why were the Bereans more noble than the Thessalonians?

    (b) In Athens, Paul noticed an altar to whom?

    (c) How was God's presence known to the Athenians?

53. Acts 18

    (a) Whom did Paul work with in Corinth before Silas and Timothy arrived?

    (b) How did God encourage Paul in Corinth?

    (c) How did Apollos help the disciples in Achaia?

54. Acts 19

(a) What happened to the seven sons of Sceva?

(b) Why did some Ephesians burn books?

(c) How did Demetrius start a riot?

55. Acts 20

(a) What happened to Eutychus?

(b) What did Paul warn the Ephesian elders about?

(c) How did the Ephesian elders show their love for Paul?

56. Acts 21:1–36

(a) What did Agabus predict about Paul?

(b) Why did Paul go to the temple?

(c) What did the Jews from Asia claim Paul was teaching against?

57. Acts 21:37—22:29   Test: Acts 16–20

(a) When Paul spoke to the angry Jerusalem crowd in Hebrew, what did he tell them?

(b) Why didn't the Romans flog Paul?

58. Acts 22:30—23:35

(a) How did Paul turn the Pharisees and Sadducees against each other?

(b) What did Paul's nephew discover?

59. Acts 24:1—25:12

(a) What did Felix do about Paul?

(b) When Felix and Drusilla spoke with Paul, what alarmed Felix?

(c) Festus asked Paul if he wished to go to Jerusalem and be tried. How did Paul respond?

60. Acts 25:13—26:32

(a) As Agrippa spoke with Festus, whom did he ask to hear?

(b) Paul asked Agrippa, "Do you believe the prophets?" How did Agrippa respond?

61. Acts 27

(a) What happened to Paul's ship as they left Crete?

(b) How did Paul encourage the people on ship?

62. Acts 28

(a) Why did the natives of Malta think Paul was a god?

(b) After three days in Rome, whom did Paul speak with?

(c) What did Paul do from his house in Rome for two years?

63. Romans 1

(a) Why wasn't Paul ashamed of the gospel?

(b) What is God's wrath revealed against?

(c) What happened to men when they did not honor God?

64. Romans 2   <u>Test</u>: Acts 21–28

(a) God will render eternal life or wrath according to what?

(b) How had Jews blasphemed God's name among the Gentiles?

65. Romans 3

(a) Who is under sin?

(b) How does righteousness come?

66. Romans 4   *Memorize* Romans 3:21–26

(a) What does the Scripture say that showed Abraham was justified by faith?

67. Romans 5:1—6:14

(a) Rarely will someone die for a righteous person. How does God show his love for Christians?

(b) If Christ's death reconciled the Christian, what did his life do?

(c) Why should the Christian be dead to sin?

68. Romans 6:15—7:25

(a) Once Christians were slaves of sin; now they are slaves of what?

(b) How did the law become death to Paul?

(c) Under the law, what did Paul desire, yet what did he do?

69. Romans 8

(a) List some differences between those who live according to the flesh and those who live according to the Spirit.

(b) What's wrong with the creation?

(c) What cannot separate the Christian from the love of God in Christ?

70. Romans 9:1–29

(a) Paul wished he were accursed for the sake of what?

(b) Being a child of God does not depend on human will or exertion but what?

71. Romans 9:30—10:21 <u>Test</u>: Romans 1–8

    (a) What parts do the heart and mouth take in salvation?

72. Romans 11

    (a) The Jews' rejection meant reconciliation for the world. What will their acceptance mean?

    (b) What places do Jews and Gentiles take in the olive tree symbol?

73. Romans 12

    (a) How should Paul's brothers present their bodies to God?

    (b) List at least three commands Paul gives the Christians in Romans 12.

74. Romans 13–14

    (a) How should everyone behave toward governing authorities?

    (b) What fulfills the law?

    (c) One person thinks it is wrong to eat meat. How should other Christians behave in his presence?

75. Romans 15 *Memorize* 1 Corinthians 13

    (a) To which kind of people did Paul like to preach the gospel?

76. Romans 16

77. 1 Corinthians 1 <u>Test</u>: Romans 9–16

    (a) What had Paul heard about the divisions in Corinth?

    (b) What is a stumbling block to Jews and folly to Gentiles?

78. 1 Corinthians 2–3

    (a) What kind of words and wisdom do the apostles teach?

    (b) What evidence showed that the Corinthians were still in the flesh?

79. 1 Corinthians 4

    (a) Who should be regarded as servants of Christ?

80. 1 Corinthians 5–6

    (a) List some sins the Corinthians committed.

(b) Whom should the Christian not associate with?

(c) What sin is committed against the body?

81. 1 Corinthians 7

(a) What did Paul teach about remaining single versus getting married?

82. 1 Corinthians 8–9

(a) What did Paul advise about food sacrificed to idols?

(b) What rightful claim did Paul and Barnabas choose not to take?

(c) Why did Paul want to preach the gospel free of charge?

83. 1 Corinthians 10

(a) What value do the Old Testament stories have?

(b) Whatever you do, do all for what?

84. 1 Corinthians 11 <u>Test</u>: 1 Corinthians 1–9

(a) What did Paul teach about head coverings?

(b) How had the Corinthians profaned the body and blood of Jesus?

85. 1 Corinthians 12–13

(a) List some Spiritual gifts.

(b) How is the human body like the body of Christ?

(c) What is the most excellent way?

86. 1 Corinthians 14

(a) Why is prophecy better than tongues?

(b) How were hymns, lessons, revelations, tongues, and interpretations delivered to the body?

87. 1 Corinthians 15

(a) What main points are in the gospel?

(b) A Christian's faith is futile if Christ hadn't been what?

(c) Those raised from the dead have what kind of body?

88. 2 Corinthians 1–2 *Memorize* 2 Corinthians 5:6–10

(a) What did Paul and Timothy experience in Asia?

(b) What feelings did Paul's previous letter cause?

89. 2 Corinthians 3–4

(a) Contrast the glory of the Old and New Covenants.

(b) List ways Paul and Timothy carried in their body the death of Jesus.

90. 2 Corinthians 5   Test: 1 Corinthians 10–15

(a) Paul spoke of a tent and a building from God. What was he talking about?

91. 2 Corinthians 6–7

(a) What events and actions commended Paul and Timothy?

(b) The coming of Titus did what for Paul and Timothy?

92. 2 Corinthians 8–9

(a) How had the Macedonian churches given for the relief of the saints?

(b) In giving, the recipient shouldn't be eased and the giver burdened, but what?

(c) God loves a ___ giver.

93. 2 Corinthians 11

(a) Paul felt divine jealousy for the Corinthians. What had happened there?

(b) List some experiences Paul boasted about.

94. 2 Corinthians 12–13

(a) Why did Paul want to boast in his weakness?

(b) How should the Corinthians test themselves?

95. Galatians 1   *Memorize* Galatians 2:17–21

(a) What astonished Paul about the Galatians?

(b) Where did Paul's gospel come from?

96. Galatians 2   Test: 2 Corinthians

(a) What did influential Jerusalem church leaders think about the gospel Paul preached?

(b) The Christian has been crucified with Christ. What kind of life does he live thereafter?

97. Galatians 3

(a) Did the Gentiles receive the Spirit by law or faith?

(b) Which covenant did the law *not* annul?

98. Galatians 4

(a) How did Hagar and Sarah symbolize the two covenants?

99. Galatians 5–6

   (a) If the Galatians accepted circumcision, of what advantage was Christ?

   (b) List some fruit of the Spirit.

   (c) Neither circumcision nor uncircumcision counts for anything. What counts?

100. Ephesians 1

   (a) List ways God blessed the Ephesians.

   (b) What did Paul pray for the Ephesians?

101. Ephesians 2–3

   (a) How is the Christian saved?

   (b) What were Christians created for?

   (c) What is the mystery of Christ revealed in chapter 3?

102. Ephesians 4   Test: Galatians

   (a) Paul says, "there is one ____, and one ____," etc. List some "ones."

   (b) What words should come from a Christian?

103. Ephesians 5   *Memorize* Ephesians 2:8–10

   (a) Who has no inheritance in the kingdom of Christ?

   (b) How should wives and husbands treat each other?

104. Ephesians 6

   (a) Describe the armor of God.

105. Philippians 1

   (a) How had Paul's imprisonment helped advance the gospel?

   (b) What was Paul pressed between?

106. Philippians 2   Test: Ephesians

   (a) How did Christ humble himself?

   (b) What had happened to Epaphroditus?

107. Philippians 3–4

   (a) Paul was a Hebrew, a Pharisee, and blameless under the law. Why did he count it as loss?

   (b) What Did Paul press on and strain for?

(c) Paul said, "Whatever is ____, whatever is ____, . . . think on these things. What things should the Philippians think on?

108. Colossians 1   *Memorize* Colossians 3:12–17

    (a) What had Paul heard about the Colossians?

    (b) List things Paul said about Christ.

109. Colossians 2

    (a) What kind of empty teaching did Paul warn about?

    (b) Instead of following the elemental teaching of the world, what should the Colossians do?

110. Colossians 3–4

    (a) What should the Christian put to death?

    (b) What should the Christian put on?

111. 1 Thessalonians 1:1—2:16

    (a) The gospel didn't just come in word. What else?

    (b) How did Paul, Silas, and Timothy live among the Thessalonians?

112. 1 Thessalonians 2:17—4:12

    (a) Why did Paul and Silas send Timothy to Thessalonica, and what did Timothy find there?

    (b) How does God want the Thessalonians to live?

    (c) Why didn't Paul need to write about brotherly love?

113. 1 Thessalonians 4:13—5:28

    (a) What happens to the dead in Christ?

    (b) When will the day of the Lord come?

    (c) List some commands Paul gave the Thessalonians at the end of 1 Thessalonians.

114. 2 Thessalonians 1:1—2:12

    (a) What will God do to those who afflict the Thessalonians?

    (b) What must come before Christ returns?

    (c) What kind of deception will Satan give the lawless one?

115. 2 Thessalonians 2:13—3:18

    (a) What did Paul command about idleness?

116. 1 Timothy 1–2

    (a) Why did Paul want Timothy to remain in Ephesus?

    (b) What saying is trustworthy and deserving of full acceptance?

    (c) What does God desire for all people?

117. 1 Timothy 3–4   <u>Test</u>: 1–2 Thessalonians

    (a) List some qualifications for overseers.

    (b) Have nothing to do with irreverent, silly myths; instead, train yourself for ____.

118. 1 Timothy 5   *Memorize* 1 Timothy 6:11–16

    (a) What commands did Paul give about widows?

    (b) What commands did Paul give about elders?

119. 1 Timothy 6

    (a) What did Paul say about riches?

    (b) What did Paul urge Timothy to pursue?

120. 2 Timothy 1

    (a) Which of Timothy's ancestors had sincere faith?

    (b) Paul lists things God does for Christians. Name some.

121. 2 Timothy 2

    (a) What should God's worker do about words, irreverent babble, and foolish controversies?

122. 2 Timothy 3–4

    (a) How will some behave in the last days?

    (b) How did Paul want Timothy to conduct his life?

    (c) Paul said, "The time of my departure has come." What was he referring to?

123. Titus 1–2

    (a) Why did Paul leave Titus in Crete?

    (b) What were some deceivers doing and teaching?

    (c) In accordance with sound doctrine, how should men and women behave?

124. Titus 3–Philemon

(a) Christians were once foolish, disobedient, and enslaved to passion and pleasure. Then what happened?

(b) What happened to Onesimus while he was away from Philemon?

(c) What did Paul want Philemon to do?

125. John 1:1–34

(a) What did the Word give to those who received him and believed in his name?

(b) What witness did John bear about Jesus?

126. John 3 Test: 2 Timothy–Philemon

(a) How can one see and enter the kingdom of God?

(b) Who has eternal life?

127. John 4:1–42

(a) What did Jesus tell the Samaritan woman about water?

(b) How do true worshipers worship the Father?

(c) The woman's testimony and Jesus' words convinced many Samaritans to do what?

128. John 6:22–71

(a) How was Jesus related to bread?

(b) No one can come to Jesus unless the Father does what?

129. John 9 *Memorize* John 3:16–18

(a) How did Jesus heal the man born blind?

(b) What did the Jewish leaders do to the man born blind?

(c) Jesus came for judgment: that the blind will see, and those who see will what?

130. John 11

(a) When Jesus arrived, how many days had Lazarus been in the tomb?

(b) Jesus said, "I am the ____ and the life. Whoever believes in me, though he die, yet shall he live."

(c) What did Jesus do for Lazarus?

131. John 13

(a) What did the feet-washing teach the disciples?

(b) What new commandment did Jesus give his disciples?

132. John 14 Test: John 1–11

(a) Thomas asked, "How can we know the way?" How did Jesus respond?

(b) Whoever has seen Jesus has seen whom?

(c) Those who love Christ keep what?

133. John 15

(a) "Whoever ____ in me and I in him, he it is that bears much fruit."

(b) "Greater love has no one that this, that someone…"

(c) How does the world feel about Jesus' disciples?

134. John 16 *Memorize* John 15:12–17

(a) After Jesus leaves, who will come?

(b) What will the Holy Spirit do?

(c) When the disciples see Jesus again, no one will take away what?

135. John 17

(a) What things did Jesus pray for his disciples?

(b) How can the world know that the Father sent Jesus?

136. John 18

(a) When the crowd said they sought Jesus of Nazareth, what did Jesus say?

(b) How did Peter enter the high priest's court?

(c) If Jesus' kingdom was of this world, what would his servants have done?

137. John 19 Test: John 13–17

(a) Pilate said, "Behold your King!" Later, the crowd responded, "We have no king but ____."

(b) What was written about Jesus on the cross?

(c) What happened after the soldier pierced Jesus' side?

138. John 20

(a) Which two disciples ran to the tomb after speaking with Mary Magdalene?

(b) The disciples were in a locked room, the evening of the first day. What happened?

(c) What made Thomas believe?

139. John 21

(a) What event occurred that made the disciple realize Jesus spoke from shore?

(b) What question did Jesus ask Simon three times?

(c) How much could be written about Jesus' works?

140. Hebrews 1–2

    (a) Long ago, God spoke through prophets. In these last days, he has spoken by whom?

    (b) Contrast the Son and angels.

    (c) What things do Christ and Christians share in common?

141. Hebrews 3:1—4:13   <u>Test</u>: John 18–21

    (a) The Hebrews writer warns his readers: "Take care lest ..."

    (b) What does the Hebrews writer say about God's rest?

142. Hebrews 4:14—6:20

    (a) Who is the Christian's high priest?

    (b) It is impossible to restore to repentance whom?

    (c) What two unchangeable things strongly encourage the Christian to hope?

143. Hebrews 9   *Memorize* Hebrews 12:1–2

    (a) What does Christ's blood do?

    (b) What did Christ do once for all?

144. Hebrews 10

    (a) Contrast Old Testament sacrifice and Christ's sacrifice.

    (b) Since Christians have confidence in Christ's blood and priesthood, what should they do?

145. Hebrews 11

    (a) Hebrews 11 lists Old Testament characters who had what?

    (b) Describe how two Old Testament characters showed faith.

146. Hebrews 12

    (a) What does the Hebrews writer say about discipline?

    (b) You have not come to a blazing fire, gloom, and a tempest, but you have come to ...

147. Hebrews 13

    (a) List three commands the Hebrews writer gives at the end of the letter.

148. James 1   *Memorize* James 3:13–18

(a) Why should Christians count trials as joy?

(b) How is someone tempted?

(c) If someone hears the word but doesn't do it, what is he like?

149. James 2 <u>Test</u>: Hebrews

(a) What does James say about partiality?

(b) What does James say about faith and works?

150. James 3–4

(a) What does James say about the tongue?

(b) What causes quarrels and fights among Christians?

(c) Instead of making plans to go a year somewhere and make money, what should you say?

151. James 5

(a) Why should the rich weep?

(b) James uses a farmer example to show Christians should be ____ until the Lord comes.

(c) Confess your sins to one another and ____ for one another, that you may be healed.

152. 1 Peter 1

(a) Christians are born again to an inheritance that is what?

(b) Do not be conformed to the passions of your former ignorance, but what?

153. 1 Peter 2 <u>Test</u>: James

(a) How is Christ like a stone?

(b) What does Peter say about suffering?

154. 1 Peter 3

(a) How should a wife adorn herself?

(b) In what manner should Christians defend in words?

155. 1 Peter 4–5

(a) Why should Christians love one another earnestly?

(b) Don't be surprised by fiery trials. Instead do what?

(c) What commands does Peter give elders?

156. 2 Peter 1

(a) What qualities did Peter want Christians to practice and increase?

(b) What evidence do we have that the power and coming of Jesus is not a myth?

157. 2 Peter 2 *Memorize* 2 Peter 1:3–8

(a) Peter uses the flood and Sodom and Gomorrah to show what?

(b) How do false teachers act?

158. 2 Peter 3

(a) What will scoffers say in the last days?

(b) The day of the Lord will come like a thief. What kind of people should Christians be?

159. 1 John 1:1—2:17

(a) God is ___, and in him there is no darkness.

(b) Whoever says, "I know Jesus," but doesn't do what he commands is what?

(c) Do not love what?

160. 1 John 2:18—3:24 Test: 1–2 Peter

(a) What does the antichrist deny?

(b) No one who abides in Christ ___.

(c) How do we know and show love?

161. 1 John 4

(a) How do you know a spirit is from God?

(b) Beloved, let us ___ one another.

(c) The presence of the Spirit, confessing that Jesus is the Son of God, and practicing love, show that we ___ in God, and God ___ in us.

162. 1 John 5

(a) What is the testimony God gave about his Son?

(b) If those who believe ask according to God's will, what can they be confident of?

163. Jude

(a) Jude urges his readers to contend for the faith. Why?

(b) Instead of causing divisions like scoffers, what should Christians do?

164. Revelation 1

(a) God gave the revelation to show his servants what?

(b) What did the man among the seven lampstands look like, and who was he?

165. Revelation 2   <u>Test</u>: 1 John and Jude

(a) List things the churches did right.

(b) List things the churches did wrong.

166. Revelation 3   *Memorize* 1 John 4:7–8

(a) What did Jesus command Sardis, the dead church?

(b) Those in Philadelphia kept Jesus' word and endured. How would Jesus help them?

(c) The church in Laodicea was neither cold nor hot. What did Jesus think about them?

167. Revelation 4–5

(a) Describe the throne in heaven.

(b) Who was worthy to open the seven-sealed scroll?

(c) What did the heavenly creatures say about the Lamb?

168. Revelation 6–7

(a) Choose two seals. Describe what happened after the Lamb opened them.

(b) Describe the scene in heaven after the 144,000 were sealed.

169. Revelation 8–9   *Memorize* Revelation 7:9–12

(a) Choose two trumpets. What happened after the angel blew the trumpet?

(b) How did the remnant of mankind react after the angels blew the trumpets?

170. Revelation 10–11

(a) How did the scroll taste?

(b) How are the two witnesses empowered?

(c) What happened after the witnesses died?

(d) What did the voices proclaim after the seventh angel blew his trumpet?

171. Revelation 12–13   <u>Test</u>: Revelation 1–9

(a) What happened to the dragon after he fought against Michael and his angels?

(b) What words did the first beast utter?

(c) What signs did the second beast perform?

172. Revelation 14–15

   (a) After the 144,000 stood on Mount Zion with the Lamb, an angel flew overhead and said what?

   (b) What did the angel do with the sharp sickle?

   (c) Those who conquered the beast, its image, and its number sang a song. Recite two phrases from it.

173. Revelation 19–20

   (a) Who judged the great prostitute and avenged on her the blood of his servants?

   (b) Describe the army that captured the beast and false prophet.

   (c) Who came to life and reigned with Christ for a thousand years?

   (d) The dead were judged according to what?

174. Revelation 21

   (a) After the first heaven and first earth pass away, where will God dwell?

   (b) Describe the new Jerusalem.

175. Revelation 22   <u>Test</u>: Revelation 10–22

   (a) What river flowed from the new Jerusalem?

   (b) When is Jesus coming?

15 Year Four Maps and Tests

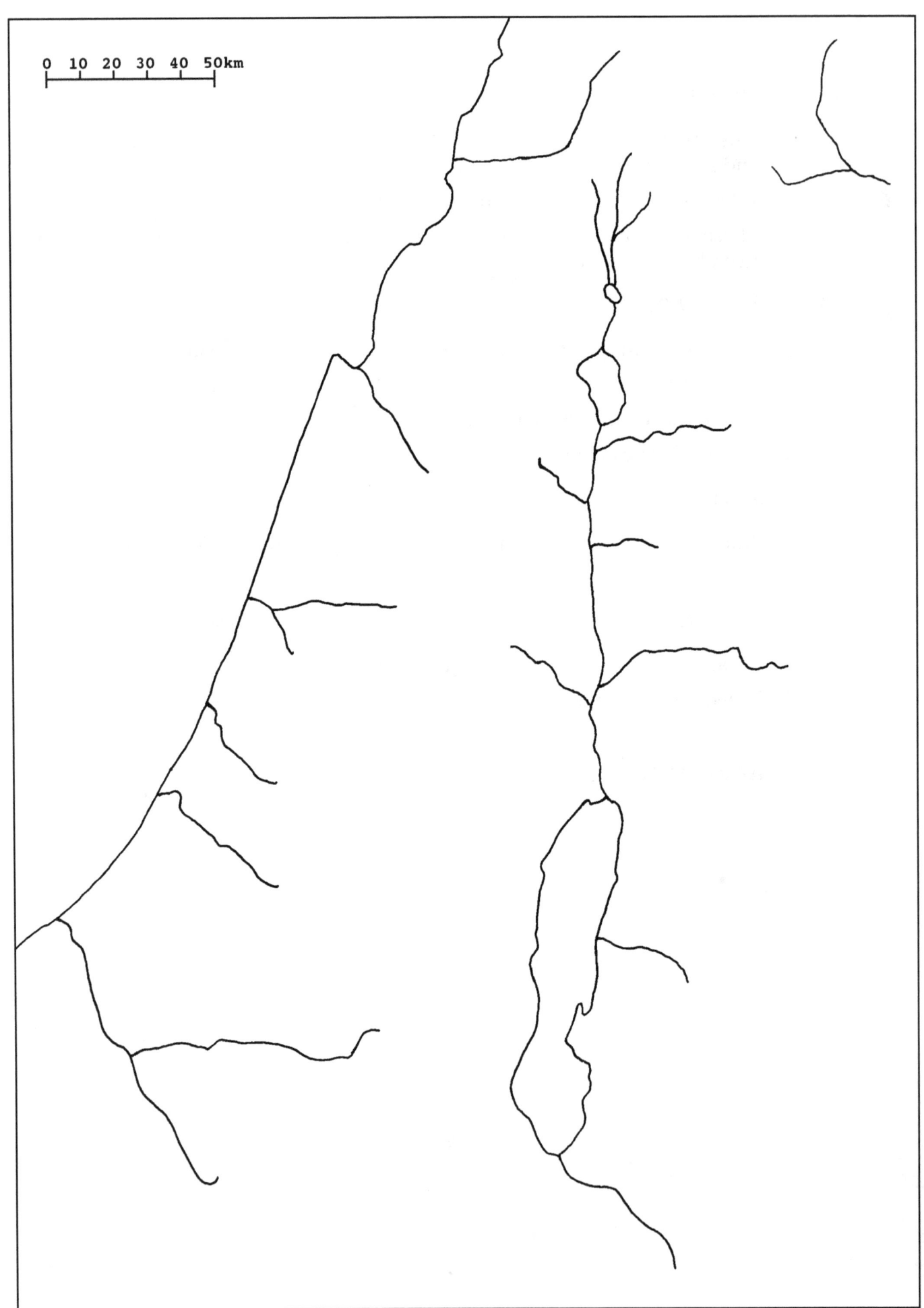

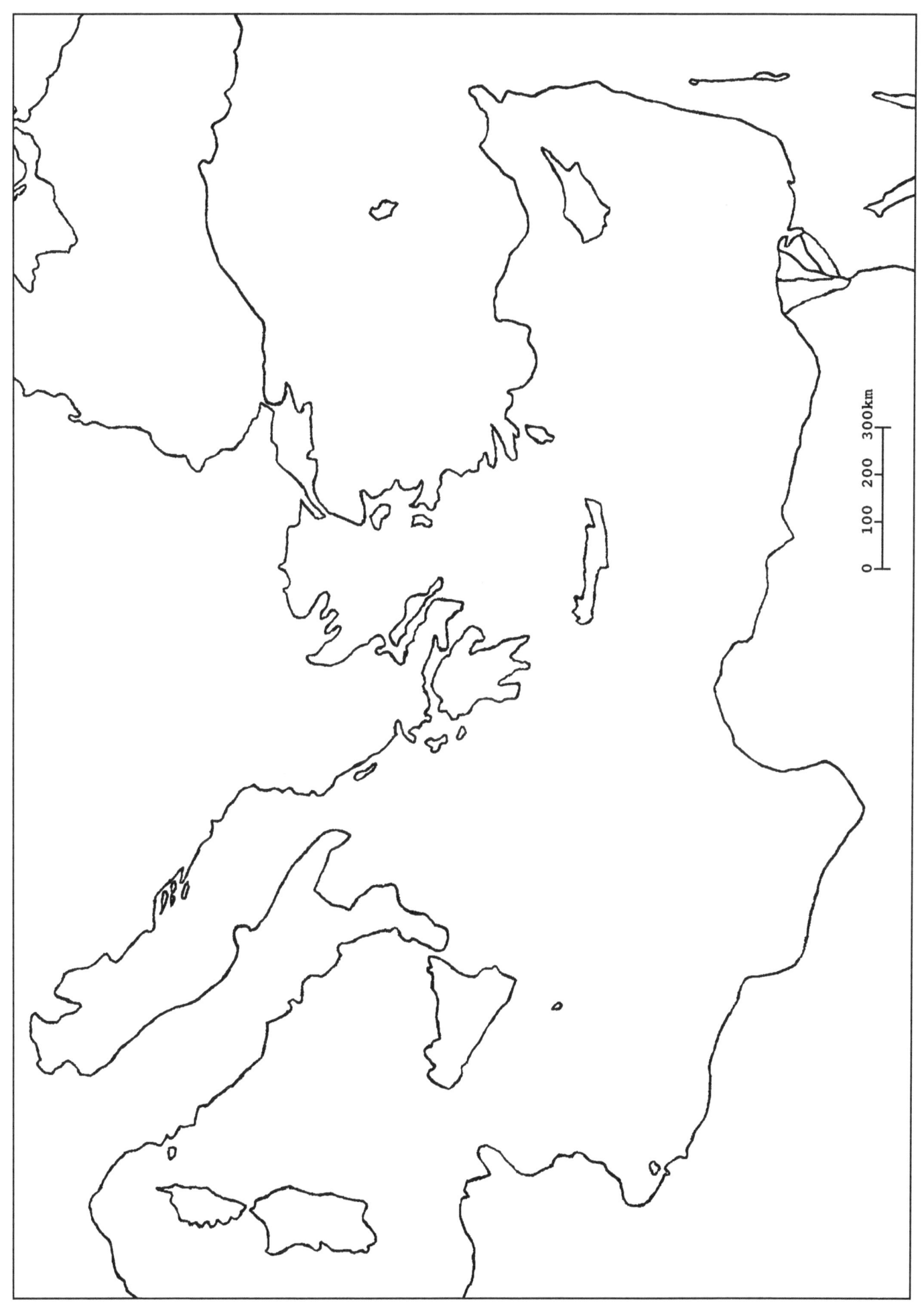

Jesus' Upbringing (Matthew 1–2, Luke 1–2)

Across
1 When Zechariah wrote, "His name is ____," his mouth was opened.
2 Gabriel told ____ she would bear Jesus.
4 Gabriel told Zechariah his wife would bear a ____.
5 To whom did the angels announce Jesus' birth?
9 Joseph and Mary came to Bethlehem to be ____.
10 Zechariah prophesied John would ____ the way for the LORD.

Down
1 Matthew records the genealogy from Abraham to whom?
3 What appeared to Zechariah in the temple?
6 When Joseph discovered Mary's pregnancy, what did he plan?
7 What did Elizabeth's baby do in the womb when Mary arrived?
8 ____ and Anna blessed and thanked God for Jesus.

Matthew 3–7

Directions: Fill in the blanks.

1. John the Baptist preached, "_____ for the kingdom of heaven is at hand."

2. When Jesus was baptized, the _____ of God descended like a dove and rested on him.

3. The devil tempted Jesus to make stones become _____, throw himself from the _____, and _____ the devil.

4. Jesus responded to the devil's temptations by quoting _____.

5. Jesus went throughout Galilee, _____, proclaiming the gospel, and healing.

6. In the Sermon on the Mount, name three groups that are blessed. _____, _____, _____

7. Jesus did not come to abolish the Law and Prophets. He came to _____ them.

8. It was said, "Whoever murders will be liable to judgment." Jesus said, "Whoever is _____ will be be liable to judgment."

9. It was said, "Love your neighbor and hate your enemy." Jesus said, "_____ your enemies."

10. Giving, prayer, and fasting should be done in _____.

11. Lay up treasures in _____.

12. Do not be anxious about what you will eat or wear. But seek first the _____ and his _____.

Matthew 8–10

Directions: Answer in complete sentences.

1. What amazed Jesus about the centurion?

2. What did Jesus do about the great storm?

3. Jesus sent out the twelve disciples. List two instructions he gave them.

4. Jesus said, "I am sending you as sheep among wolves." What did he predict men would do?

5. Jesus said, "I have not come to bring peace, but a sword." List two groups who are not worthy of Jesus.

Matthew 11–14

```
A D I U U Z L V L I N N R K A H
S P G I U Y G S M C R H J L G D
G T W Y G Y Q T E H P O R P Y Y
K M A C E T L M H R E J L N H V
M L L N A G K G X O O B D M W A
N F K Y D R G E N E R A T I O N
B H E S D E E W L B N N H W R G
S N D C X A X P J C J M S E K P
C A Q E W T M Z E J D O I F S P
E M S R A E H D K T Y E F V G Y
V A C K T R L S A B B A T H C R
```

1. Jesus told ___ ___ ___ ___, "The blind receive sight, the lame walk, lepers are cleansed, the deaf hear, the dead are raised, and the poor have good news preached to them."

2. Among those born of women there has arisen none ___ ___ ___ ___ ___ ___ ___ than John the Baptist.

3. Woe to Chorazin and Bethsaida! For if the mighty ___ ___ ___ ___ ___ done in you had been done in Tyre and Sidon, they would have repented.

4. The Pharisees criticized Jesus disciples for plucking grain on the ___ ___ ___ ___ ___ ___ ___.

5. Jesus reminded the Pharisees that David ate the bread of the Presence and the priests profane the Sabbath. Something greater than the ___ ___ ___ ___ ___ ___ ___ is here.

6. The Pharisees believed Jesus cast out demons by Beelzebul. Jesus said a kingdom divided against itself will not __ __ __ __ __.

7. At the judgment, the men of Nineveh will condemn this __ __ __ __ __ __ __ __ __ because they repented at the preaching of Jonah, and something greater than Jonah is here.

8. Seed fell on the path, on rocky ground, among __ __ __ __ __ __, and on good soil.

9. The seed sown on good soil represents the one who __ __ __ __ __ the word and understands it.

10. __ __ __ __ __ came up among the grain. The __ __ __ __ __ are the sons of the evil one.

11. A __ __ __ __ __ __ __ is without honor in his hometown.

12. After Herodias's daughter __ __ __ __ __ __ for Herod, he had John beheaded.

13. Jesus fed a large crowd with five loaves and two __ __ __ __.

14. Peter __ __ __ __ __ __ on the water with Jesus.

Matthew 15–18

Directions: Circle the letter of the best answer.

1. The Pharisees broke God's commandment for what?

    (a) money
    (b) family
    (c) tradition
    (d) power

2. What defiles a person?

    (a) what comes out of the mouth
    (b) what goes in the mouth
    (c) leprosy
    (d) eating with sinners

3. Jesus asked, "Who do you say that I am?" How did Peter reply?

    (a) "You are the Christ, the Son of the living God."
    (b) "You are a great teacher."
    (c) "You are a prophet."
    (d) "You are John the Baptist."

4. If someone would come after Jesus, what must he do?

    (a) fast, eat clean food, and sacrifice
    (b) study, avoid folly, and teach
    (c) satisfy desire, try his best, and store up treasures on earth
    (d) deny himself, take up his cross, and follow Jesus

5. Jesus took Peter, James, and John up a high mountain. What did they see?

    (a) a beautiful view
    (b) Jesus shining and talking with Moses and Elijah
    (c) a large crowd
    (d) the devil

6. Jesus said, "Elijah has already come." Of whom was he speaking?

    (a) Herod
    (b) John
    (c) Mary
    (d) Zechariah

7. Who is the greatest in the kingdom of heaven?

    (a) he who humbles himself like a child
    (b) he who gives all to the poor
    (c) he who heals the sick
    (d) he who brings the most to Christ

8. How many times should you forgive a brother who sins against you?

    (a) 1
    (b) 7
    (c) 100
    (d) 70x7

9. Jesus told a story of a king and debtors. Why should you forgive your brother from your heart?

    (a) because his sin wasn't too bad

    (b) because he didn't mean to harm

    (c) because God forgave me a greater debt

    (d) because sin is a small problem

10. There is joy in heaven over a sinner who does what?

    (a) stops sinning

    (b) starts doing right

    (c) repents

    (d) befriends God

11. What did the prodigal do with his share of the property?

    (a) squandered it

    (b) invested it

    (c) gave it away

    (d) built a tower

12. When the prodigal returned, how did his father greet him?

    (a) He said, "I told you so."

    (b) He refused to see him.

    (c) He sent his servant to care for him.

    (d) He hugged and kissed him.

13. Why did the master commend the dishonest manager?

    (a) because the master liked dishonesty

    (b) because the manager acted shrewdly

    (c) because the manager became honest

    (d) because the manager shared the master's money with the poor

14. If people do not hear Moses and the Prophets, neither will they be convinced if

    (a) Jesus performed miracles

    (b) someone should rise from the dead

    (c) their parents were Christians

    (d) an angel appeared to them

Matthew 19–22

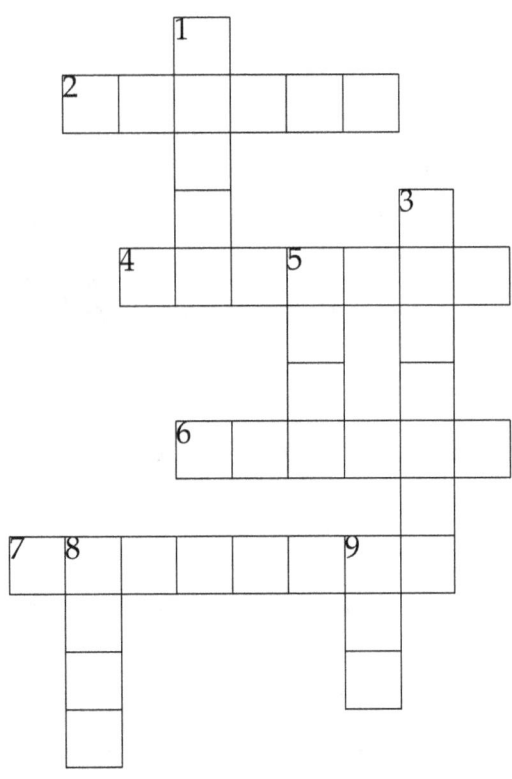

Across

2 Jesus overturned the money-changers' tables, saying, "My house shall be called a house of ____, but you make it a den of robbers."

4 The crowds shouted, "____ is he who comes in the name of the Lord!"

6 Render to ____ the things that are Caesar's.

7 "You shall love the Lord your God with all your heart and with all your soul and with all your mind" is the ____ commandment.

Down

1 It is easier for a ____ to go through the eye of a needle than for a rich person to enter the kingdom of God.

3 Whoever would be great among you must be your ____.

5 The all-day laborers and the last-hour laborers received the ____ pay.

8 Jesus told the ____ man, "Sell what you have, give to the poor, and come, follow me."

9 The tenants murdered the vineyard owner's ____.

Matthew 23–25

Jesus said, "Woe to you, scribes and Pharisees." List at least three things the scribes and Pharisees did wrong.

What things will happen toward the end of the age? List at least three things.

What was the difference between the sheep and the goats? Be specific about what they did.

Matthew 26–28

Directions: Fill in the blanks.

1. The woman poured ointment on Jesus' head. The _____ said it was wasteful. Jesus, however, said she had done a _____ thing.

2. The bread meant _____.

3. The wine meant _____.

4. Before he was captured, Jesus went to Gethsemane and _____.

5. Judas betrayed Jesus with a _____.

6. The scribes and Council put Jesus on trial. They wanted evidence that they might _____.

7. A servant girl said Peter was with Jesus, but Peter _____ it.

8. After Jesus was condemned, Judas returned the money and then _____ himself.

9. Which prisoner did the crowd choose to release? _____

10. Pilate _____ his hands before the crowd, saying, "I am innocent of this man's blood."

11. The passers-by, the priests, the scribes, and the elders _____ Jesus while he was on the cross.

12. After Jesus' death, the _____ of the temple was torn in two, from top to bottom.

13. The chief priests secured the tomb by sealing the _____ and setting a _____.

14. When _____ Magdalene and the other _____ went to the tomb, they met an angel.

15. The angel told the women, "Do not be afraid . . . He has _____."

16. Before Jesus departed, he commanded the disciples to make disciples, baptize, and _____ his commandments.

Acts 1–5

Directions: Answer in complete sentences.

1. How did Jesus leave earth?

2. Who replaced Judas?

3. How did the Holy Spirit come at Pentecost?

4. According to Peter what had God done to Jesus, and what had the people done to Jesus?

5. What did Peter and John give the lame man at the Beautiful Gate?

6. By what power did Peter and John heal the lame man?

7. The high priest and elders commanded Peter and John not to speak in the name of Jesus anymore. How did Peter and John reply?

8. After Peter and John were released, for what did the believers pray?

9. Why did Ananias and Sapphira die?

10. Why did people bring the sick to the apostles?

Acts 6–10

```
H  P  D  F  M  O  V  N  L  B  C
L  Z  A  J  L  B  A  J  B  N  J
P  J  M  O  N  E  Y  O  S  K  P
H  H  A  H  L  S  X  S  X  J  T
Y  R  S  C  A  T  T  E  R  E  D
B  W  C  P  P  W  U  P  E  G  G
V  J  U  J  I  D  X  H  S  Q  V
H  O  S  D  L  R  S  O  I  Q  E
L  P  O  Y  I  W  I  X  S  Q  Z
Z  W  M  X  H  L  U  T  T  S  A
S  N  E  H  P  E  T  S  T  W  Y
```

1. Some _ _ _ _ _ _ were neglected in the daily distribution, so the disciples appointed seven men to serve.

2. _ _ _ _ _ _ _ spoke wisely and by the Spirit; some from the synagogue of the Freedmen could not stand it.

3. God chose _ _ _ _ _ _ _ and Moses, but the Israelites rejected them.

4. Stephen said the Jews always _ _ _ _ _ _ _ the Holy Spirit.

5. After Stephen's death, the church was _ _ _ _ _ _ _ _ _ throughout Judea and Samaria.

6. Peter rebuked Simon, because Simon thought he could obtain the gift of God with _ _ _ _ _ .

7. _ _ _ _ _ _ told the Ethiopian the good news about Jesus.

8. On the road to _ _ _ _ _ _ _ _, Jesus spoke with Saul, and Saul was blinded.

9. In a trance, Peter saw a _ _ _ _ _ with unclean animals in it.

10. In Peter's trance, a voice said, "What God has made _ _ _ _ _, do not call common."

11. While Peter spoke about Jesus to Cornelius's household, the Holy _ _ _ _ _ _ fell on them.

Acts 11–15

Directions: Circle the letter of the best answer.

1. Who rescued Peter from prison?
   (a) Herod
   (b) an angel
   (c) John
   (d) Caesar

2. People shouted that Herod was a god. Why did Herod die?
   (a) He did not give God the glory.
   (b) Someone assassinated him.
   (c) Old age took him.
   (d) God wanted him glorified.

3. Paul said Bar-Jesus, the magician in Cyprus, was
   (a) a powerful man.
   (b) near to the kingdom.
   (c) foolish.
   (d) a son of the devil.

4. Who spoke to the crowd in Antioch in Pisidia?
   (a) Paul
   (b) Barnabas
   (c) Peter
   (d) James

5. How did the Jews in Antioch in Pisidia respond?
   (a) Some believed.
   (b) Some reviled Paul.
   (c) Some were filled with jealousy.
   (d) all of the above

6. The people in Lystra treated Barnabas and Paul as gods after they saw what?
   (a) lightning in the sky
   (b) the dead rise
   (c) a lame man walk
   (d) a blind man see

7. As they returned to Lystra, Iconium and Antioch, what did Barnabas and Paul *not* do?
   (a) made peace with the Jews
   (b) strengthened
   (c) encouraged
   (d) warned of tribulation

8. What did some in Judea teach the brothers in Antioch?
   (a) the law of Moses
   (b) the proverbs of Solomon
   (c) You must be circumcised to be saved.
   (d) Jesus did not rise.

9. What ruling did the leaders in Jerusalem *not* deliver to the Gentiles?
   (a) They should abstain from sexual immorality.
   (b) They should be circumcised.
   (c) They should abstain from food sacrificed to idols.
   (d) They should abstain from blood.

10. How did the Jerusalem leaders make their decision known?

    (a) They wrote a letter.

    (b) They sent Judas and Silas.

    (c) both (a) and (b)

    (d) none of the above

Acts 16–20

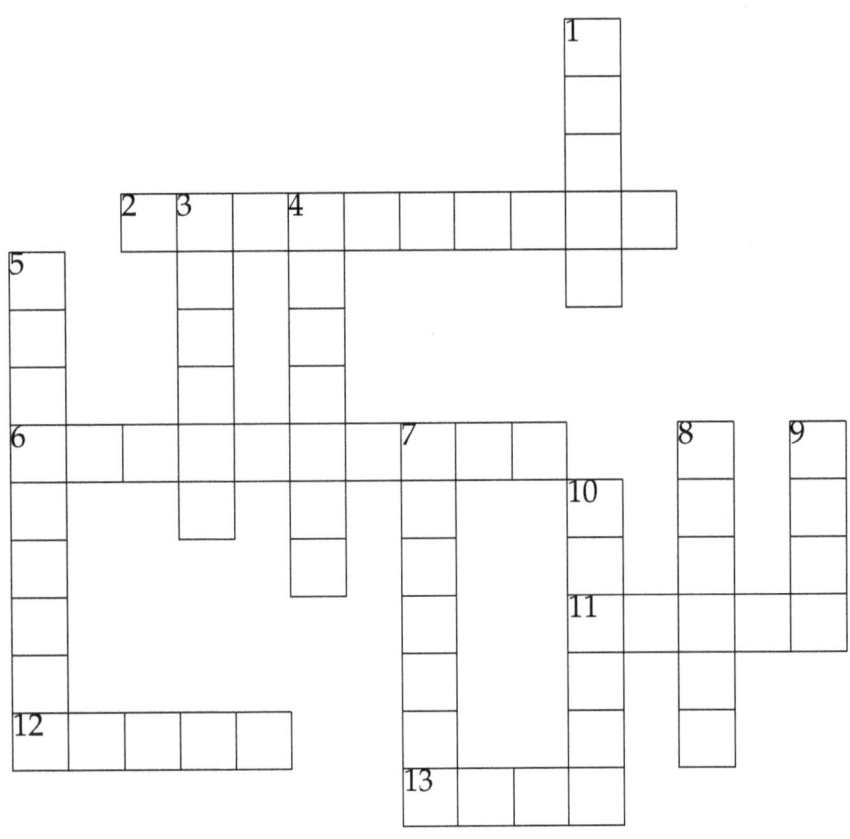

Across

2 As Paul and Silas sang in jail, there was an ____.

6 The Bereans examined the ____ daily to see if Paul's and Silas's words were true.

11 The ____ sons of Sceva cast out spirits in Jesus' name. They suffered for it, because they didn't know Jesus.

12 In Athens, Paul found an ____ to an unknown god.

13 As Paul spoke on, Eutychus fell asleep and ____.

Down

1 The Ephesians burned their magic ____.

3 In Corinth, God told Paul, "Do not be ____."

4 Paul and Silas met ____ in Lystra. He accompanied them on their journey.

5 In Corinth, Paul worked with ____ and Aquila.

7 Apollos powerfully ____ the Jews in public.

8 Paul warned the Ephesians that ____ will come among them.

9 Paul cast out a spirit in Philippi. The girl's owners saw their hope for ____ was gone.

10 The Ephesians wept and hugged and ____ Paul.

Acts 21–28

In Acts 22–26, Paul speaks before crowds and Roman leaders. Write about one of those times. Summarize Paul's words and the crowds' or leaders' reactions.

Tell the story about Paul's voyage from Crete to Malta. Use at least 5 sentences.

331

Romans 1–8

Directions: Fill in the blanks.

1. Paul wasn't ashamed of the _____ because it was the power of God for salvation to everyone who believes.

2. God's _____ is revealed against all ungodliness and unrighteousness of men.

3. Men did not honor God; therefore, God _____ to impurity.

4. God will render _____ to those who do good.

5. Those who _____ the law blasphemed God's name among the Gentiles.

6. All have _____ and fall short of the glory of God.

7. God revealed a righteousness that comes through _____.

8. Abraham wasn't justified by works. The Scripture says, "Abraham _____ God, and it was counted to him as righteousness."

9. "God shows his _____ for us in that while we were still sinners, Christ died for us."

10. The Christian is _____ to sin.

11. Once you were slaves of sin; now, you are slaves of _____.

12. Under the law, Paul wanted to do _____, but he was weakened by the flesh.

13. The mind set on the _____ is death, but the mind set on the _____ is life and peace.

14. Nothing can separate the Christian from the _____ of God in Christ.

Romans 9–16

```
S  X  H  T  U  O  M  Q  O  P
W  A  O  N  W  S  Q  S  A  W
C  X  C  U  T  C  E  U  J  A
E  Y  C  R  N  L  L  P  W  T
H  V  L  O  I  I  F  M  L  C
X  R  O  T  B  F  R  E  F  E
Z  E  N  L  O  E  I  R  N  J
K  E  G  V  S  U  I  C  D  B
G  O  O  D  C  B  R  Y  E  U
X  S  T  U  M  B  L  E  P  S
```

1. Paul wished he were accursed and ___ ___ ___ off for the sake of the Israelites.

2. Being a child of God does not depend on human will or exertion but on God's ___ ___ ___ ___ ___ ___.

3. With the heart one believes and is justified, and with the ___ ___ ___ ___ ___ one confesses and is saved.

4. Israel's rejection meant reconciliation for all; their acceptance meant ___ ___ ___ ___ from the dead.

5. The ___ ___ ___ ___ ___ ___ ___ ___ are like wild olive shoots grafted into a cultivated olive tree.

6. Paul's brothers should present their bodies as living ___ ___ ___ ___ ___ ___ ___ ___ ___.

7. Do not be overcome by evil, but overcome evil with ___ ___ ___ ___.

8. Let every person be _ _ _ _ _ _ _ to the governing authorities.

9. _ _ _ _ fulfills the law.

10. It is good not to eat meat or drink wine or do anything that causes your brother to _ _ _ _ _ _ _.

11. _ _ _ _ made it his ambition to preach the gospel where Christ was not named.

1 Corinthians 1–9

Directions: Answer in complete sentences.

1. What had Paul heard about the divisions in Corinth?

2. What is a stumbling block to Jews and folly to Gentiles?

3. What kind of words and wisdom do the apostles teach?

4. What evidence showed that the Corinthians were still in the flesh?

5. List some sins the Corinthians committed.

6. Whom should the Christian not associate with?

7. What sin is committed against the body?

8. What did Paul teach about remaining single versus getting married?

_____

_____

_____

_____

9. What did Paul advise about food sacrificed to idols?

_____

_____

10. What rightful claim did Paul and Barnabas choose not to take?

_____

_____

1 Corinthians 10–15

Directions: Circle the letter of the best answer.

1. The Old Testament stories
   (a) have no use today.
   (b) are for the Jews only.
   (c) were written for the Christian's instruction.
   (d) should be studied in literature classes.

2. Whatever you do, do all for
   (a) the glory of God.
   (b) the benefit of others.
   (c) the poor and needy.
   (d) yourself.

3. Concerning head coverings, Paul said
   (a) men should wear them, women should not
   (b) women should wear them, men should not
   (c) all should wear them
   (d) none should wear them

4. How had the Corinthians profaned the body and blood of Jesus?
   (a) idolatry
   (b) sexual immorality
   (c) getting drunk at the Lord's supper
   (d) law suits

5. Spiritual gifts are
   (a) prophecy
   (b) healing
   (c) teaching
   (d) all of the above

6. Paul compares the human body to the body of Christ. Which comparison does he *not* make?
   (a) Each has different parts but they are all needed.
   (b) Weaker members are indispensable.
   (c) If one member suffers, all suffer together.
   (d) It can survive without an arm.

7. What is the most excellent way?
   (a) the way of the Spirit
   (b) love
   (c) knowledge
   (d) charity

8. Prophecy is better than tongues because it
   (a) builds up the church.
   (b) takes more of the Spirit.
   (c) serves as a sign to non-believers.
   (d) is more ancient.

9. The main points of the gospel are

   (a) Those who do right inherit eternal life; those who do wrong inherit eternal punishment.

   (b) All sin. Sacrifice brings reconciliation.

   (c) Christ died for our sins. Christ was buried. Christ rose.

   (d) All sin. Christ's birth saves.

10. A Christian's faith is futile if

    (a) they disobey the Law of Moses.

    (b) Christ had not been raised.

    (c) Christ had not performed miracles.

    (d) they sin.

2 Corinthians

Across

2 The churches in _____ gave generously.
5 Paul contrasts our earthly body, a _____, with our heavenly body, a building from God.
8 Paul and Timothy commended themselves with afflictions, _____, beatings, imprisonments, and hunger.
9 Paul's previous letter caused pain and _____.
10 Paul _____ about his Israelite lineage, imprisonments, beatings and dangers.
11 The New Covenant exceeds the Old covenant in _____.

Down

1 Christ's power is made perfect in _____.
3 God loves a _____ giver.
4 Paul and Timothy were afflicted, but not crushed; struck down, but not destroyed; always carrying in the body the _____ of Jesus.
6 Paul and _____ experienced such affliction in Asia, they despaired of life.
7 God comforted Paul and Timothy with the coming of _____.

Galatians

How were the Galatians turning to a different gospel?

What was the purpose of the law?

Contrast the works of the flesh and the fruit of the Spirit.

Ephesians

Directions: Fill in the blanks.

1. God blessed the Ephesians by _____ and _____.

2. Paul prayed God would give the Ephesians a spirit of wisdom and revelation that they may know _____ and _____.

3. "For by _____ you have been saved through _____."

4. "We are his workmanship, created in Christ Jesus for _____."

5. The _____ of Christ is that the Gentiles are united with the Jews through the gospel.

6. There is one _____, one _____ and one _____.

7. "Let no corrupting talk come out of your mouths, but only such as is good for _____."

8. The _____ have no inheritance in the kingdom of Christ.

9. Wives should _____ to their husbands; husbands should _____ their wives.

10. Take up the armor of God: the _____ and the _____.

Philippians and Colossians

```
U E P A P H R O D I T U S S
F V Y W N L E P S O G S J S
M E P L I R C R O J O T Z E
B R Y F P D O R P L O Y K N
V Y E W I E N H E U V S E D
T T Q X P L C B M A M L J N
O H W C H R I S T P T F Q I
G I I D D M L J W O B E M K
U N V N D D E A T H U O D S
L G J H K H D D E L B M U H
```

1. Paul's imprisonment helped advance the __ __ __ __ __ __ .

2. Paul was pressed between __ __ __ __ and death. There were benefits to each.

3. Christ __ __ __ __ __ __ __ himself by becoming a man and dying.

4. __ __ __ __ __ __ __ __ __ __ __ __, the Philippians' messenger and minister to Paul, became sick and nearly died.

5. Being a Hebrew, a Pharisee, and blameless under the law was __ __ __ __ compared to knowing Christ.

6. Whatever is true, whatever is just, whatever is lovely, __ __ __ __ __ about these things.

7. By Christ, all things were __ __ __ __ __ __ __ .

8. Christ is above __ __ __ __ __ __ __ __ __ .

343

9. Christ _ _ _ _ _ _ _ _ _ _ to himself all things.

10. _ _ _ _ warned about following the regulations of the elemental spirits of the world which say, "Do not handle, Do not taste, Do not touch."

11. Instead of following the elemental spirits of the world, be rooted in _ _ _ _ _ _ _.

12. Put to _ _ _ _ _ sexual immorality, impurity, passion, evil desire and covetousness.

13. Put on compassion, _ _ _ _ _ _ _ _, humility, meekness, and patience.

1–2 Thessalonians

Directions: Answer in complete sentences.

1. The gospel didn't just come in word. What else?

2. How did Paul, Silas, and Timothy live among the Thessalonians?

3. Why did Paul and Silas send Timothy to Thessalonica, and what did Timothy find there?

4. Why didn't Paul need to write about brotherly love?

5. What happens to the dead in Christ?

6. When will the day of the Lord come?

7. List some commands Paul gave the Thessalonians at the end of 1 Thessalonians.

8. What must come before Christ returns?

   _____

   _____

9. What kind of deception will Satan give the lawless one?

   _____

   _____

10. What did Paul command about idleness?

    _____

    _____

1 Timothy

Directions: Circle the letter of the best answer.

1. Why did Paul want Timothy to remain in Ephesus?

    (a) to charge some not to teach different doctrines

    (b) to raise up young believers

    (c) to help the church endure persecution

    (d) to appoint elders

2. What saying is trustworthy and deserving of full acceptance?

    (a) All have sinned and fall short of the glory of God.

    (b) The LORD works righteousness and justice for the oppressed.

    (c) Christ Jesus came into the world to save sinners.

    (d) The righteous inherit eternal life.

3. What does God desire for all people?

    (a) food

    (b) salvation

    (c) happiness

    (d) possessions

4. What is *not* a qualification for an overseer?

    (a) sober-minded

    (b) able to teach

    (c) hospitable

    (d) strong

5. Have nothing to do with irreverent, silly myths; instead, train yourself for

    (a) heaven.

    (b) godliness.

    (c) school.

    (d) wisdom.

6. Which qualification was *not* necessary for widows to be enrolled?

    (a) She must teach children.

    (b) She must be 60 or older.

    (c) She must have a reputation for good works.

    (d) She must have no children.

7. Elders are worthy of

    (a) church money.

    (b) nothing.

    (c) not being rebuked.

    (d) double honor.

8. Those who desire to be rich

    (a) aim for a worthy goal.

    (b) must work hard.

    (c) fall into temptation.

    (d) may be elders.

9. Pursue

    (a) righteousness.

    (b) love.

    (c) gentleness.

    (d) all of the above

2 Timothy, Titus, Philemon

Across
2 Before God saved them, Christians were foolish, disobedient, and enslaved to ___ and pleasures.
4 ___ in what you have learned and believed.
7 In the last days, people will appear ___, but deny its power.
8 Timothy's grandmother and ___ had sincere faith.
9 While away from Philemon, ___ became a Christian.
10 ___ said, "The time of my departure has come." He knew he would soon die.
11 ___ were teaching for shameful gain and devoting themselves to Jewish myths.

Down
1 ___ saved Christians and called them to a holy calling.
3 ___ irreverent babble and foolish controversies.
4 Men and women should be self-___.
5 Paul left Titus in Crete to put things in order and appoint ___.
6 Paul wanted Philemon to ___ Onesimus as he would receive Paul.

John 1–11

Directions: Fill in the blanks.

1. To all who received him, and believed in his name, he gave the right to become _____ of God.

2. _____ said, "This is the Son of God."

3. No one can see the kingdom of God unless he is _____.

4. Whoever _____ in him should not perish but have eternal life.

5. The _____ Jesus gives wells up to eternal life.

6. True worshipers worship in spirit and _____.

7. Many _____ believed because of the woman's words and Jesus' words.

8. Jesus is the bread of _____.

9. No one can come to Jesus unless the Father _____ him.

10. Jesus spat, made mud, and healed the _____ man.

11. Jesus came for _____: that the blind may see and the seeing may become blind.

12. When Jesus arrived, Lazarus had been in the tomb _____ days.

13. Jesus said, "I am the _____ and the life. Whoever believes in me, though he die, yet shall he live."

John 13–17

```
C  C  X  G  R  E  A  T  E  R  V  N
K  O  O  V  M  P  X  S  V  D  T  P
J  D  M  U  K  W  E  L  Z  A  R  S
T  O  J  M  F  T  U  O  O  A  M  M
C  Y  W  T  A  U  Z  N  Y  O  J  Y
I  C  F  H  T  N  M  E  M  G  B  L
V  W  A  S  H  E  D  P  D  O  I  T
N  F  B  O  E  K  U  M  R  F  A  I
O  R  I  L  R  C  K  K  E  T  Z  R
C  I  D  N  O  V  C  Y  Q  N  U  I
Q  Y  E  D  K  V  H  T  U  R  T  P
B  Y  S  C  A  N  E  M  Q  T  T  S
```

1. If Jesus, their Teacher and Lord, _ _ _ _ _ _ their feet, they should do the same for one another.

2. Jesus gave a new commandment: "_ _ _ _ one another as I have loved you."

3. Jesus is the way, the truth, and the _ _ _ _ _.

4. Whoever has seen Jesus has seen the _ _ _ _ _ _.

5. Those who love Christ keep his _ _ _ _ _ _ _ _ _ _ _ _.

6. Whoever _ _ _ _ _ _ in me and I in him bears much fruit.

7. _ _ _ _ _ _ _ love has no one than this, that someone lays down his life for his friends.

8. The world _ _ _ _ _ Jesus' disciples.

350

9. After Jesus goes away, the _ _ _ _ _ _ of truth will come.

10. The Spirit will _ _ _ _ _ _ _ the world concerning sin, righteousness, and judgment.

11. The Spirit will guide Jesus' disciples into all _ _ _ _ _.

12. When the disciples see Jesus again, no one will take away their _ _ _.

13. Jesus _ _ _ _ _ _ for his disciples, asking the Father to keep them in his name, to sanctify them in the truth, and that they may all be one.

14. Jesus asked that his followers be _ _ _, so the world may believe that God sent Jesus.

John 18–21

Directions: Answer in complete sentences.

1. When the crowd said they sought Jesus of Nazareth, what did Jesus say?

2. How did Peter enter the high priest's court?

3. If Jesus' kingdom was of this world, what would his servants have done?

4. Pilate said, "Behold your King!" How did the crowd respond?

5. What was written about Jesus on the cross?

6. What happened after the soldier pierced Jesus' side?

7. Which two disciples ran to the tomb after speaking with Mary Magdalene?

8. The disciples were in a locked room, the evening of the first day. What happened?

9. What made Thomas believe?

10. What event occurred that made the disciple realize Jesus spoke from shore?

11. What question did Jesus ask Simon three times?

12. How much could be written about Jesus works?

Hebrews

The Hebrews writer contrasts Christ and the Old Covenant. Be specific, and explain further.

Describe two Old Testament characters' faith. How, therefore, should the Christian act?

James

Directions: Fill in the blanks.

1. Count it joy when you meet _____.

2. Each one is _____ by his own desire.

3. Someone who hears the word but doesn't do it is like someone who looks in a _____ and forgets what he was like.

4. Show no _____ between rich and poor.

5. Faith apart from _____ is dead.

6. The _____ is a restless evil, full of deadly poison.

7. Your _____ at war within you cause quarrels and fights among you.

8. Instead of saying, "I will go and spend a year and make money," you should say, "If the _____ wills, I will live and do this or that."

9. The _____ should weep and howl, because miseries are coming. They held back wages and lived in luxury and self-indulgence.

10. In the same manner that the farmer waits for crops, be _____ until the Lord's coming.

11. Confess your sins to one another and _____ for one another, that you may be healed.

1–2 Peter

```
E E K E F L H T I A F W I
P G X C M N C F L D S F L
P O N N O P R O P H E T S
B D N A D M G E O D E E U
R L J T O P I L J A G A F
J I B I S I Y N C O W E F
M N V R M R O H G V I E E
D E F E N S E U S E V C R
E S T H X R V D K O E W E
K S E N S D S T L U S Z D
X Y M I G S T O N E K O N
```

1. Christians are born again to an __ __ __ __ __ __ __ __ __ __ that is imperishable, undefiled, and unfading.

2. Do not be conformed to the passions of your former ignorance but be __ __ __ __, as God is __ __ __ __.

3. Christ is like a __ __ __ __ __. Men rejected and stumbled over it, but God chose it.

4. Christ __ __ __ __ __ __ __ __, and Christians follow in his steps.

5. __ __ __ __ __ should adorn themselves with the hidden person of the heart and a gentle and quiet spirit.

6. Be prepared to make a __ __ __ __ __ __ __, but do it with gentleness and respect.

7. __ __ __ __ covers a multitude of sins.

8. Do not be surprised at fiery trials; instead, _ _ _ _ _ _ _.

9. _ _ _ _ _ _ should shepherd willingly, eagerly, and humbly.

10. Supplement your _ _ _ _ _ with virtue, knowledge, self-control, steadfastness, godliness, brotherly affection, and love.

11. Jesus' power and coming is not a myth. The apostles witnessed it, and the _ _ _ _ _ _ _ predicted it.

12. Peter used the flood and _ _ _ _ _ and Gomorrah to show that God spares the righteous and punishes the wicked.

13. False _ _ _ _ _ _ _ _ bring heresy, exploit listeners, blaspheme God, and live sinfully.

14. In the last days, scoffers will ask, "Where is the promise of his _ _ _ _ _ _?"

15. The day of the Lord will come like a thief. Christians should live lives of holiness and _ _ _ _ _ _ _ _ _.

1 John and Jude

Directions: Answer in complete sentences.

1. God is what, and in him there is no darkness?

2. Whoever says, "I know Jesus" but doesn't do what he commands is what?

3. Do not love what?

4. What does the antichrist deny?

5. No one who abides in Christ does what?

6. How do we know and show love?

7. How do you know a spirit is from God?

8. Beloved, let us do what to one another?

9. The presence of the Spirit, confessing that Jesus is the Son of God, and practicing love, show what about God and us?

10. What is the testimony God gave about his Son?

11. If those who believe ask according to God's will, what can they be confident of?

12. Jude urges his readers to contend for the faith. Why?

13. Instead of causing divisions like scoffers, what should Christians do?

Revelation 1–9

Directions: Circle the letter of the best answer.

1. God gave the revelation to show his servants what

    (a) they did wrong.
    (b) must soon take place.
    (c) their enemies planned.
    (d) Christ desired.

2. The man with hair like wool, eyes like fire, and feet like bronze that stood among the lampstands was

    (a) Gabriel
    (b) the antichrist
    (c) Christ
    (d) Satan

3. The church in Pergamum, where Satan had his throne, held fast Jesus' name and did not deny the faith, but had some who

    (a) taught others to eat food sacrificed to idols.
    (b) taught others to practice sexual immorality.
    (c) held the teaching of the Nicolatians.
    (d) all of the above

4. Christ commanded Sardis, the dead church, to

    (a) remember what you received, keep it, and repent.
    (b) cease meeting.
    (c) hear the new teaching, and do it.
    (d) get over it and act alive.

5. The church in Philadelphia kept Jesus' word and endured. Therefore,

    (a) Jesus would keep them from the hour of trial.
    (b) Jesus would test them harder.
    (c) Jesus would give them a break.
    (d) Jesus would grant them prosperity.

6. What did *not* happen around the throne in heaven?

    (a) Four living creatures said, "Holy, holy, holy, is the Lord God Almighty."
    (b) Sacrifices were offered continually.
    (c) 24 elders sat on 24 thrones.
    (d) Lightning and thunder came from the throne.

7. Who was worthy to open the seven-sealed scroll?

    (a) John
    (b) Michael
    (c) Abraham
    (d) the Lamb

8. What part was *not* in the song sung by the creatures and elders?

    (a) You punish the wicked.
    (b) Worthy are you to take the scroll.
    (c) By your blood you ransomed people for God.
    (d) You made the ransomed a kingdom of priests to reign on the earth.

9. After he opened the second seal,

    (a) a pink horse came, and the rider afflicted men with sunburn.

    (b) a red horse came, and the rider took peace from the earth.

    (c) a green horse came, and the rider scattered weeds among the crops.

    (d) a blue horse came, and the rider destroyed the earth with flood.

10. After they sealed the 144,000, what did John *not* see in heaven?

    (a) a great multitude clothed in white crying, "Salvation belongs to our God and to the Lamb!"

    (b) the angels, elders, and creatures falling on their faces and worshipping

    (c) the angels, elders, and creatures saying, "Blessing, glory, wisdom, honor, power, and might be to our God forever."

    (d) all mankind giving honor to the Lamb.

11. After the third angel blew his trumpet, a star fell from heaven and

    (a) struck Jupiter

    (b) frightened the nations

    (c) fell on the rivers and springs

    (d) turned into Satan

12. After the sixth trumpet plagues, the rest of mankind

    (a) did not repent.

    (b) hid among caves.

    (c) repented.

    (d) fought each other.

Revelation 10–22

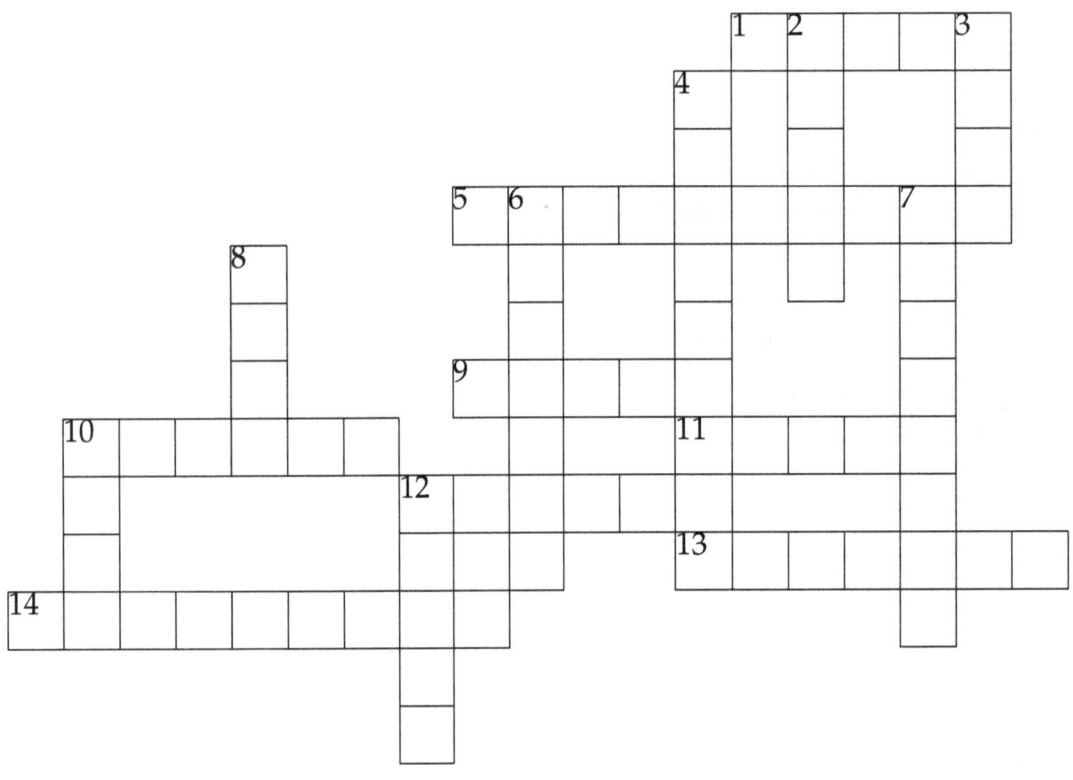

Across

1 After the first heaven and earth pass away, God will _____ with man.
5 God judged the great _____ and avenged on her the blood of his servants.
9 The first beast utters blasphemous _____.
10 After the _____ fought against Michael and his angels, he was thrown down to earth.
11 The second beast performs great _____.
12 The angel reaped the harvest of the earth with his _____.
13 After the _____ angel blew his trumpet, loud voices said, "The kingdom of the world has become the kingdom of our Lord and of his Christ."
14 An angel showed John the Bride, the new _____.

Down

2 The one called Faithful and True rode a _____ horse.
3 The river of _____ flowed from the throne of God.
4 The two _____ were empowered to shut the sky, turn waters to blood, and strike the earth with plague.
6 People will _____ over the witnesses' death, but three and a half days later the witnesses will rise.
7 Those beheaded for the testimony of Jesus came to life and reigned with Christ for a _____ years.
8 Those who conquered the beast, its image, and its number sang a _____.
10 The dead were judged according to what they had _____.
12 The scroll tasted _____ but was bitter to the stomach.